Paris Made Me…

by John Kirby Abraham

The type-style font chosen for the word "Paris" on the cover is the creation of Alfons Mucha, the celebrated arte nouveau artist born in Movaria who worked and exhibited in Germany and France in the 1930's.

Order this book online at www.trafford.com
or email orders@trafford.com

Most Trafford titles are also available at major online book retailers.

Printed in Victoria, BC, Canada.

ISBN: 978-1-4251-2211-9

Our mission is to efficiently provide the world's finest, most comprehensive book publishing service, enabling every author to experience success. To find out how to publish your book, your way, and have it available worldwide, visit us online at www.trafford.com

Trafford rev. 4/2/10

 www.trafford.com

North America & international
toll-free: 1 888 232 4444 (USA & Canada)
phone: 250 383 6864 ♦ fax: 812 355 4082

THE AUTHOR EXPRESSES GRATEFUL thanks to Lynn Jeffress, Charles Mercier and Krystyna Prusik for their professional assistance and photographer Meredith Mullins for the cover photograph.

Chapter 1

"There are two worlds; the world that we can measure with line and rule, and the world we can feel with our hearts and imaginations."

Leigh Hunt, The Story of Rimini essayist & poet (1784-1859)

A GROWING BUT INTERMITTENT awareness that there are two worlds, not only one, has troubled me for some time. One is the tangible world we see and hear and touch. The other is in the mind and does not conform to the senses I once tidily catalogued for my students in the desert. It is a world of conflicting moods, of dark turmoil and wide inviting vistas, of shining objectives, but sometimes of black despair. This other world bears not the slightest resemblance to everyday existence and appears totally independent of it, or so it seems to me.

One day, when walking down the wet Parisian street outside the house to buy some bread, I had this momentary feeling of elation and strength, of endless possibilities that owed nothing to the immediate environment. And so I resolved, as I have recently often resolved, to try to put into words my thoughts and feelings on this subject. And therein lies my initial difficulty.

I use words every day in my job, but my words evaporate from the moment they are spoken. George Orwell in Nineteen-Eighty-Four warned us of the danger of "newspeak" and "doublethink." My fear is that anything I begin to express in written words will immediately fall short of what I want to describe. And yet I have to start, because that is what I resolved to do when walking down the street to buy some bread.

The Story Begins --

The long adventure began one winter in Hampstead, in my room overlooking the great grey city of London. Anne-Marie had brought a precious record for me to hear. We sat on the floor in front of the gas-fire listening to the passionate singing voice of Jacques Brel, the Belgian singer who had conquered France just as Anne-Marie had conquered me. When she left to join her family in East Africa, we promised that we would meet somewhere in the coming year.

And so I left my youthful world of effort and achievement in England and travelled far to meet her on an island. Does it matter now that we never met again, that other loves would claim me, shame me, on Mediterranean shores? Even my later meetings with the likes of Brel, when I came to rest in France, could never equal the adventures unleashed by Anne-Marie in London.

In 1967, I found myself living in the eastern Paris suburb of Bagnolet, as the guest of two female friends living in a street with the propitious name, Rue de la Liberté. For a modest wage, I worked three times a week on the night-shift in the French State radio station, presenting an early morning news bulletin in English for listeners to the overseas service.

Paris presented an unfamiliar aspect of desolation and quiet when I drove into the capital at one o'clock in the morning. The wide avenues were deserted and the lines of street lamps shone on the shiny road surface. The Seine flowed serenely under the bridges and there was a mystical atmosphere in the air.

The huge round radio station standing on the banks of the river was brilliantly lit as though for a party, but inside it seemed almost deserted except for night-workers like myself. Even the night-porter's head was barely visible behind his desk as I took the lift to our offices. The workplace was similar to many others, stale smelling, untidy, with discarded paper everywhere. The telex machines were manned by a nearly toothless old man who bellowed greetings to me over the clatter of dispatches spilling on to the floor. I gathered up wads of raw material of world events and went to work at my desk. I was happy to enter this closed world like a giant ocean liner sailing through the night.

Given established guidelines, composing a news bulletin was not difficult. I quickly pursued familiar long-running stories and seized upon urgent new ones. "De Gaulle vetoes Britain's entry into the European Common Market…France launches its first nuclear submarine…the Vietnam War rages on…and, a Picasso picture was sold at auction in London for half-a-million dollars!" (A world record for the work of a living artist!) With the digital clock marking the minutes to air-time, there was neither a moment or a place for editorial comment or subtleties of verbal expression. In the studio, in front of a yawning technician, I firmly addressed the microphone at 6:15am and my words were instantly winging their way into space. When I finally left the building, the pale tints of dawn were already streaking the sky beyond the Eiffel Tower. While Paris was awakening, half my day had already ended. It was twilight at dawn as Baudelaire once wrote…

L'aurore grelottante en robe rose et verte
S'avancait lentement sur la Seine désert,
Et le sombre Paris, en se frottant les yeux,
Empoignait ses outils, viellard laborieux.

Charles Baudelaire (1821-1867) Le Crépuscule du matin

Back in the real world of Bagnolet, I recounted the latest news to Maryse and Elizabeth over breakfast before they left for their respective jobs in the city. Although I was informed of the latest French and international news, little of my night's work seemed to have any relevance to our day-to-day existence. We lived simply and comfortably, each of us contributed to our daily needs. With a small income, I had a feeling of inferiority living with two working girls. I was haunted by the recent theft of my personal belongings in Vienna when returning to Europe. I was ashamed to eat and would go out and sit in the public gardens or a church when it was cold or raining. I knew almost nothing about the world below our windows. Alone in the flat once more, I reflected on recent events that had brought me to France.

It had begun in Copenhagen a day after Christmas. I was sitting in the sun behind white lace curtains listening to Grieg. The dusty record turned and Solveig's plaintive song from "Peer Gynt" came distantly through the dry heat of the room. For a few fugitive moments, I was floating among the puff-balls of white cloud that decorated the Danish sky that day. I was in an anguish of pleasure remembering other skies, in earlier years, when warm Mediterranean winds had brought strange sounds to a mountainside where I had lain among rocks and herbs…. The music induced a moment of timelessness….

Suddenly Maiken came out of the bathroom wrapped in a purple towel and said, "Let's open a window, it's so hot in here!" And I said, "Better wait a bit. You'll catch cold if you do that." But she opened the window anyway. The record came to an end and the machine shut off with a click. I said, "I think I'll make a cup of tea." And that was the end of it; a sudden realisation that everything we had lived in recent months across Europe was finished. What was I doing filming the marriage of Queen Margrethe II to Count Henri de Laborde in the church of Holmens Kirke in Copenhagen with an Ariflex camera on my shoulder? Even my brief stint as a cameraman could not keep me in Denmark now that Maryse had invited me to join her in Paris. Within a week, I was on the road to France to begin all over again.

Diary entry -

I remembered the surging ocean, when as a soldier on board the troop-ship we came to rest in Egypt. Then I remembered the waves sucking and curling round the rocks on the island of Cyprus. There I found a cosmos of lost souls, living their last days before revolution and Republic. Later I moved to the sights and smells of Beirut, a foreign world so strange I could have come from Mars. Survival in a mediaeval world of money and misery seemed to be the pattern of the Near East. A sweep through Europe brought me to clean, simple Denmark where cattle grazed in green fields and the world was young again. What silly thoughts one has on a winter's afternoon when the sun is dying behind the rooftops in Paris.

My first job in Paris had been at the International Edition of the New York Times, in offices in the Rue de Berri, near the veteran Le Figaro newspaper. What I did not know was that due to competition from the Herald Tribune-Washington Post, the Times edition was due to close and my brief sales efforts as Head of Promotion were fore-doomed. I was honourably paid off and regretfully filed the earlier letters of welcome I had received from the parent paper in New York. The rival International Herald Tribune prospered beside a dozen French newspapers and a few imported non-French dailies. An English ex-army acquaintance informed me that the French State radio was looking for English speakers for their overseas service. That was my next stop.

From my temporary home in Bagnolet, before sleeping after my night's work at the radio station, I went down to shop in the near-by open-air street market. As I mingled with the crowds pressing in all directions, a great melody filled my head, a slow dance of people surging this way and that, not knowing which way to turn. Why was I there at that time and place? Like all the others I had joined the dance but most of my being was not yet present. It was soaring above the crowd like a bird looking for a nesting place.

I returned to our house in the suburbs with food supplies and then slept, later to await Maryse's return, to hear her foot-tapping on the stairs and her key in the lock. I thought of her upturned eyes and humourous smile and presence that had come to mean so much to me by inviting me to Paris. It had begun long ago in the Mediterranean when we once tried to leave the shore and swim to another land. Now it was different; no sun, sea or rocks, just cliffs of buildings and streets of sound. If I could penetrate those wide brown eyes, I could lose myself in them forever. But I also knew I would soon leave our house and find a home of my own, nearer to my new place of work at the radio station.

Belleville

Belleville is perched on an east Paris hillside.

At the crossroads of four Parisian communes, Belleville was once a small hillside village near Montmartre housing 65,000 people. It retained the shape and character it held before being annexed to Paris in 1860. One day, I walked into a Paris I did not know. It was a quarter of crumbling old dwellings in steep cobbled streets with such names as Rue de Peking and Senegal Passage. Belleville was annexed to the capital when the former fortified walls were raised under Louis Philippe. Reputedly slightly higher than Montmartre, Belleville also had its vines and wines to refresh a mixed population of different nationalities and origins. It had become a cradle of cabarets and cafés that had nurtured such talents as Maurice Chevalier and Edith Piaf. I sat observing the roofs of the city and imagined the thousands inside the business offices and workshops that kept the capital turning. Then I returned to our suburb to await the return of Maryse and Elizabeth to know if anything was needed in the kitchen.

We did occasionally leave our "palace" in Bagnolet with Elizabeth's friend Alan. There was a day when we left the Paris region. It was not warm but bright and sunny. We wrapped up and laughed inside of Alan's old Citroen car. The last ugly houses and posters sped by and we soon found ourselves in the country. We ran among tall grass like children out of school and sat on a fallen tree and ate chicken legs with our fingers and became a little drunk on cheap red wine. There were no shadows that day. The clouds were so distant they could not be seen and could never, ever touch us, or so it seemed that spring day. The dusty faded photograph taken by a man with a gun, as we stood together on the fallen tree and raised our glasses to a single fleeting moment in our lives, Maryse had pinned it up in the kitchen as a token reminder of a moment of a day of happiness.

Maryse and author spending a day in the country.

Perhaps the sweetest time of all was an evening in Paris when we sat in the open air at opposite sides of a small table and spoke. I hardly noticed what we ate or drank. Everything she said was open and frank. She said she thought she loved him. And when she was with him, she loved him. I said I thought there was no more hope for us. Not so much truth had fallen from our lips for a very long time. Now it was over. "It will pass. You will forget!" I said. She actually smiled, the first I had seen for many weeks.

But it was already too late and long past the allotted time for such words. Of course it will pass, as all the others will pass into the frozen store of memories. But the wound will be there still. We embraced before parting and resumed the role of two people out for an evening stroll. We were as two travellers in two separate trains that had stopped at the same station and then pulled away in opposite directions. I had turned a new page in a life half spent.

Chapter 2

"Most of our life is like a blind man sleepwalking. For the greater part, which is, I suppose, the best part, we are unaware that this immediate step will lead in that direction. Drifting from triviality to frivolity we allow the pressure of circumstances to mount until we are driven one way or another. We seldom have to bear the burden of decision and when we take one, we are often quite unconscious of having done so."

Ronald Duncan, How To Make Enemies 1968

IN THE AUTUMN, I rented a small room in the 15th district of Paris near the river. My sixth-floor "studio" with a terrace, looked out over zinc roofs and chimneys towards the distant hills of Meudon. Below was a corner of wasteland where homeless "clochards" and stray dogs lived in peaceful harmony next to a stable of donkeys which were led each day to the public gardens to offer children rides. It was a friendly district where local shopkeepers stood gossiping in their doorways when business was slow. Not far away, the surface Métro trains clanked up and down the Boulevard de Grenelle on grey iron supports. The other side of the line was unfamiliar ground. The quarter reflected an epoch when Vaugirard and Grenelle were still villages.

I must have been the only person working in the radio station who did not possess a television. I did have a fixed telephone which enabled those in charge to summon me to work an extra nightshift or a weekend or by an urgent "pneumatic" communication. After a short walk up the Rue du Theatre to a temporary footbridge spanning the

Seine, I entered the great round Office de Radio Télévision Française, the ORTF, known familiarly as the "camembert" after the round, boxed Norman cheeses.

French State Radio Station built in 1963.

The ORTF, inaugurated by President de Gaulle in 1963, comprised eleven kilometres of corridors serving some seventy production studios encircling a central tower which housed the archives. Several thousand people toiled day and night producing news, information and entertainment in several languages for national and foreign services. The recent introduction of the first SECAM colour television channel had added pressure of office-space within the vast rotunda.

My initiation as a radio journalist had been casual, not to say cursory. Presenting myself at an initial meeting, I was given a French Press Agency dispatch to translate and type into English. As I struggled to rapidly make sense of the report, the head of the service put a friendly hand on my shoulder and said, "That's fine! Now come and have a drink!" Across the street in the Télé Bar, I was introduced to other members of his team. It was Old Burge's way of screening newcomers to the English language service. As the son of a celebrated Irish poet, he had been with De Gaulle in London during the war and was to become my mentor in the coming years and the radio station my second home. A new chapter of my Paris life had begun.

Alone in my cocoon in the heart of the city, my thoughts returned to the flat-land I had so recently left. A page from my diary brought to life a day spent with M in Sealand: "It was late summer. We went to visit a small, still lake set among low folds of a meadowland. Trying to capture some effects of sunlight on the water with my camera, I stalked through the long grass beside the water. M followed, bored, sucking grass stalks and sweeping the low bushes with a stick. We passed through several fields where cows were contentedly grazing. Then the bull came at us marching from the farthest corner of the field as we arrived in the middle. M screamed and we both ran. We reached the edge of the field, the great brown animal lumbering after us. After crawling under a wire fence, we collapsed panting and laughing in the long grass, looking up at the great beast's indignant expression. It stood staring at us then turned back to his cows. Then we slept until the sun died behind the trees and the lake. The whole flat earth was still and we possessed it that afternoon. We motored home flushed and smiling without a single word. Time was running out for both of us.... Would it still be there today? I doubt it. The country of the mind is vast and ever-changing like the billows of the sea."

I had arrived in Paris at the right time to savour the evolution of France under the 5th Republic. The country was still basking in the glow of relative post-war affluence. Living was cheap, car ownership was wide-spread, summer vacations and winter ski holidays were common and many urban families enjoyed a second home in the country. In December, half a million Parisians left by train alone to spend Christmas in the mountains or by the sea.

President Charles de Gaulle was at the height of his power, if not popularity. Following a visit to the Soviet Union, De Gaulle had made an official visit to the Canadian province of Quebec as guest of the Federal Government, a country composed of two different ethnic communities. His provocative public declaration in French, "Vive le Quebec libre!" implying pre-eminence of the French language, made from a balcony in Montreal, caused a sensation. At home, despite an agreement over agricultural policy among the members of the six European Common

Market countries, De Gaulle continued to cast doubts over Britain's true intentions. Meanwhile, the first Franco-British supersonic passenger aircraft was completed in the southern French city of Toulouse, with a minor flurry over whether the name Concorde should be spelt with or without the French feminine 'e.' France prevailed over the issue.

De Gaulle's return to the capital often offered him the chance to drive down the Champs Elysées standing in an open vehicle like a Roman Emperor, to receive applause from the anonymous crowds constantly wandering down the avenue. A press conference at the Elysée Palace was a further opportunity for him to play the part of a national leader commenting on the state of the world. With my new accreditation as journalist, I began to take my place among French and foreign correspondents in well-rehearsed demonstrations of French political life in action.

Morning editorial conferences attended by all language services at the radio station offered guidelines on the subject and treatment of news and information to be broadcast from Paris. The English service presented the world as seen from France, with the added attraction of French events and personalities. As I sat with my colleagues taking notes, the sight of the Eiffel Tower visible from our windows reminded me of the evolution of radio communications. Our programmes were carried world-wide from the summit of the tower that was once the tallest in the world and had since become the symbol of France. I had entered the hub of a French international communications network.

Ever since he had rallied French Resistance forces in broadcasts from the BBC in London during the war, De Gaulle understood the value of communication by radio and television. Decolonization was well underway and France needed to maintain and nurture friendly relations with her former overseas territories. Britain, Belgium and Portugal were developing their foreign radio services for the same reason and the Voice of America was already omnipresent on several continents. Other industrialised countries such as the Soviet Union, Germany and Japan were developing their foreign language services. Radio Luxembourg claimed many listeners in Europe. The principality of Monaco had Radio Monaco to defend its neutral independent status within France's frontiers. Britain's independent Radio Caroline was already broadcasting offshore from the North Sea in the 1960's. The ORTF, a French state monopoly since its creation in 1944, addressed the French nation and overseas departments and audiences through medium and shortwave radio programs from Paris, relayed by transmitters abroad. The global war of the airwaves by satellites had hardly yet begun.

Radio communication was increasingly recognized as an ideal medium for informing, educating and motivating people. Radio and television could cross frontiers and reach both a mass market and isolated regions. The rivalry of languages and dialects in Third World countries was growing. Developing countries were the scene of a growing rivalry between industrial nations for economic or political reasons. Due to uncertain levels of literacy, audio-visual communication was more easily accessible than the written press for reasons of language differences and distribution.

Africa was still a relatively virgin territory to receive foreign sound and images, notably from the U.S., Britain, Germany and France. While the Voice of America, Germany and the BBC flooded the African continent. France had set up two relay stations in Africa, in the Congo Brazzaville and Gabon. Others were planned in Latin America. Meanwhile the Soviet Union headed the list of foreign language broadcasts (seventy languages against thirty-five for the V.O.A. and thirty-six from the BBC, while the French ORTF stood at only fifteen languages.) In terms of broadcasting hours, Radio Moscow far outran the V.O.A. and the BBC, leaving the ORTF in Paris at the bottom of the list.

Reading about the mounting sickness of many capitalist and industrialist societies, I realised that these must be considered halcyon days compared with what was to come. France had barely begun to react to the growing problems of the switch from an agricultural to an industrial economy. At the same time she was playing the old diplomatic game with her friends and neighbours based on obsolete rules and outworn protocol. Despite the continuing mood of post-war euphoria, Labour Unions had begun political protests against the government's project to legislate financial problems by decree, thus bypassing Parliament. De Gaulle had already lost his overall majority in the National Assembly but stoutly defended the actions of his chosen Prime Minister Georges Pompidou, whom he considered to be a man of rare intelligence.

Protests were also beginning to erupt over the urban developments of the capital. Despite the decision of the Cultural Affairs Minister, André Malraux, to wash clean historic buildings, Paris had begun to look more like a grey-faced hag than a spring-fresh Marianne. There was talk of the planned removal of Les Halles, the wholesale food market, from the centre of the capital. The eight centuries old food market, originally set up by King Philippe Auguste in 1183, called the "Belly of Paris" by the eminent writer Emile Zola, was originally designed to cater for one and half million people. Lately, it had been attempting to feed more than eight million inhabitants of the Paris region. The future of Victor Baltard's twelve huge iron and glass pavilions housing the market remained uncertain.

At an exhibition in the Decorative Arts Museum of the proposed development of the seventy acre market site, I talked to Social Affairs Minister, Edgar Faure about the fate of the historic pavilions. I asked him if they would be sold for scrap or re-erected somewhere else as testimony of an earlier age when the Eiffel Tower was built. The Minister could not give an answer to my question. A letter published in the International Herald Tribune in Paris stated pertinently, "It should not be beyond the ingenuity of the French State planners to devise a way of preserving at least four of the celebrated structures of Baltard which are threatened by destruction." My fifteen-page illustrated article about developments in the French capital was published in the London Geographical Magazine and a photo was accepted for the Canadian Toronto Daily Star.

The vast documentation and sound archives in the radio station offered unlimited sources of French culture and history. When I was not on duty preparing the latest news, I contented myself at home with music and song. My small battery-powered record player brought alive the singing voices of Charles Trenet, Catherine Sauvage, Edith Piaf and many others. The songs of Maurice Chevalier recalled the time when he first strode the music-hall stage and made films in Hollywood. When his characteristic voice intoned, "Every little breeze seems to whisper Louise, birds in the trees seem to twitter Louise...." I mentally replaced the song title with the name Maryse, the words so perfectly expressed my latent feelings for she who had brought me to Paris.

We continued to meet occasionally. Maryse brought me a friendly postcard from the writer Lawrence Durrell, now living in the south of France. He regretted that a new deadline for his forthcoming book made an interview difficult at the moment. I recalled when we were on the island of Cyprus together and he was finishing his Alexandria Quartet. A man of many parts, poet, novelist and British Press Attaché abroad, Durrell had once concluded a family dinner party at his home in England by inviting me to see some of his recent paintings, before returning to the Mediterranean he loved. On a visit to a Paris theatre to see Tom Stoppard's play Rosencrantz and Guildenstern are Dead, the Czech author's first play about two characters in Shakespeare's Hamlet, Maryse and I suddenly found ourselves sitting next to Durrell near the front stalls! A few months later I found him signing his latest book for customers in the Shakespeare and Company bookshop in the Latin Quarter.

In our fifth-floor office in the radio station, we had been joined by a young French West Indian journalist, Marie-Claude Celeste. A dedicated third-world observer, she had come to Europe from Guadeloupe to study Political Science and perfect her English. After a brief spell with the BBC in London she had joined our team at a time when France's concerns were with its former overseas territories. Marie-Claude quickly found her vocation producing a weekly Spotlight on Africa programme, while also contributing to the French publication Jeune Afrique destined for African immigrants.

Winter passed. Spring emerged, slowly and with effort. The skies cleared, the rain ceased and suddenly one morning there was golden sunlight on the roofs. The skyline changed very little in this quarter of the city. The solid houses stood like cliffs through which the narrow streets seemed carved with a knife. The only thing that changed was the sky, an ever changing pattern of colour and cloud that moved or raced across the rooftops. As I looked out from this little sun-trap of grey stone, I saw only concrete walls and roofs stretching away in jagged waves to the south and west. And then would come a rare still day when the sky would attain an almost uniform blue seen through a thin gauze of "townsmell." And the memories of other days in other climates would come seeping back to me.

At home in my room in the clouds, the echo of a woodpecker comes in on the soft spring air, it could be from a forest clearing. But sadness of sadness, I know there is but one tree in the whole of this locality standing in a wide clearing where there was once a garden and a house. It is perhaps the last tree in the whole quarter, not even flourishing any more but standing dying and waiting for the axe. I shall be sorry, though, about the tree. Each early morning and evening for the past weeks a bird has sung a sweet and lucid song from its dead branches, so penetrating and clear that it filled the whole sleeping district with its voice. Watching the branches bend under the wind in a surge of unrest, I realise once again that the catalogue of all we feel is in nature and we simply seek out those aspects that best reflect our innermost feelings. Thus artists, creators, draw upon the scenes around them to express in words, sounds, movement and colours, what is within them. There lies the true secret of art, poetry, music...and thought! To recognise what is within one and give it shape, movement, meaning! The rest is waste.

My thoughts returned again and again to the island of Cyprus. I found this strange because Paris is so many people's dream. It was also once vaguely mine, although until my late thirties I had not begun to acquire the necessary knowledge to appreciate French life and culture. A rare morning, for example, when crossing the Pont des Arts, I sat facing the Ile de la Cité, the traffic's distant rumble on either side of me, below the sparkling River Seine. A thrumming river-boat passed below the bridge, a couple stood in the bows, single persons stood on the bridge, transfixed in thought, watching, wondering....

The clear egg-shell blue sky was delicately tinted towards the east, joining white buildings on either bank. I wanted to join the river, lapping, laughing on its way to the sea. I was once in the prow of boat, surging towards unknown destinations. I remembered days at sea, drumming eastwards through the Mediterranean....

There was a time when we danced on board ship and the people we saw each day suddenly looked different and the band played softly in the warm night air. When the dance was over, we sat on abandoned deck-chairs and listened to the thud of the engines and the faint hiss of wash astern. The smoke from the funnel looked white in the bright starlit night. The sky was like velvet you could touch and caress.

Someone stood beside me at the rail and placed their hand on mine and we exchanged glances. As we looked down at the water, there were flashes of phosphor in the waves. The ship shuddered and everyone went to sleep. Our cabin was warm and stuffy.

Next morning, the crew was washing down the corridors and the passengers looked worried about what time we would reach port and if their families and friends would meet them. Someone you had known every day for two weeks at the dinner table, passed without a nod. Stewards looked with renewed interest at departing passengers and became over-polite. The place where we had danced the night before looked bright and inhospitable like a coloured photograph in a travel brochure.

Soon we sighted low hills. As we drew near to the port, the land-mist cleared to reveal houses, trees and people. The sound of the engines ceased and we entered shallow water. We splashed ashore under the gaze of people waiting to unload the ship. There was bustle and movement as we left our temporary home at sea for firm ground, smells, sounds and sensations of a new strange land. So this was Cyprus, the Island of Love! Aphrodite had chosen well! All that came back to me as I stood on the bridge in Paris watching a river-boat pushing aside the waters of the Seine. And I never knew her name!

Chapter 3

La vie est un sommeil,
l'amour en est le réve,
Et vous aurez vécu si vous avez aimé.

Alfred de Musset (1810-1857)

ANOTHER DAY OF EFFORT expended by brain and voice in the service of radio, playing the part of a newsreader and commentator. Authoritative, well-balanced phrases, a touch of humour to match the content, but facts had to respected and reported. The news of the day poured endlessly out of the teleprinters.

Some events reminded me of places I had once known. Today, the International Committee of the Red Cross confirmed that hundreds of Palestinians had been massacred in two refugee camps in West Beirut. My thoughts fled back to Lebanon between the mountains and the sea and the ancient city of Baalbek where I had once taken part in an international music festival in the Roman temple of Bacchus. The Lebanese writer Khalil Gibran, once wrote, «Je suis voyageur et navigateur. Et tous les jours, je découvre un nouveau continent dans les profondeurs de mon ame.» (I am a traveller and navigator and every day I discover a new continent in the depths of my soul .)

Back to the news of the day: the world's first space-man, Colonel Youri Gagarine of Russia was killed in a Mig 15 trainer plane accident and in France, to accommodate a growing nine million inhabitants in the Paris region, eight new satellite towns are to be set up by the year

2000. And still in France, residents of the distant Alpine village of Cruseille fought to protect their hundred year old fountain in the village square from demolition from bulldozers. When the work-force arrived to prepare a new traffic island, their church bells sounded the alarm. Police quickly restored order and the fountain was saved.

After duty, I am out in the cool street, across the river and home to my hole in the sky. The glow of the sun illuminates the wall, the city's hum and throb is behind the window and I return to the real world of imagination. I prepare a pot of tea, eat eggs, honey and an apple. Then I sit and survey this small, over-lit room that is my temporary home. What does temporary mean if I am spending some of my life here? More can happen in a minute than in a year.

Virginia, a radio colleague, telephoned and made that peculiar "tutting" noise which meant she was uncertain what to say. I responded with my usual shallow, empty good humour. While I was talking to her, I was telling myself not to make any suggestion that we meet, because it would have ended as all the other meetings have ended. She rang off without my having asked her to lunch. I sat in the chair for half an hour listening to the dying echo of our conversation and wondering if I had not put another nail in my head.

My nearest neighbour was a man whom I rarely saw, closed in his room on our common terrace. A second neighbour was a young woman who had lost no time in inviting me in for a drink when I had arrived in the house. Her small room was richly decorated like a grotto with coloured cushions and fairy lights and flowers. She remained a friendly but discrete neighbour. Meanwhile, the world beyond my window remained still largely unexplored.

In spite of the excitement and challenge of my life in Paris, I felt unfulfilled and my thoughts returned to my island, the country I had adopted after London. There in the Mediterranean, I had experienced both a sense of peace and also of furious activity, of living almost to the maximum of my potential. I remembered the round of seasons that gave life a continuity and shape. Long winter days of rain when storm clouds exploded and poured their contents over villages and plain, giving way to a veritable rebirth that was the spring. Then there was the rush to the mountains and the sea, and I was in love and loved. The image of those days of restless energy remain precious and intact, like a live thing waiting to be released. Now Paris, city of so many people's dreams, it was also once mine before I had acquired the necessary knowledge to appreciate and question French life and culture.

Our team of journalists was composed of some twenty men and women of varied backgrounds and origins. They now included Simon, a young English student of the Etienne Decroux Mime School, who had theatrical ambitions and a young woman named Spoutnik from India named after the Soviet first earth-orbiting space satellite launched in 1957. Did she know that her first name meant "comrade" or "fellow traveller" in Russian? We were supported by production assistants, technicians and an administrative staff and a network of foreign correspondents. A tight rota system, not including preparation of recorded features and interviews, ensured our physical presence in the studio to conduct more than thirty live broadcasts each week.

The huge round radio station beside the Seine was like a small city housing several thousand men and women daily including visitors and invited guests. Like Charlie Chaplin in Modern Times, we were little different from factory employees at a conveyer belt. While the media machine turned day and night, personal relationships often flourished in the corridors or at the coffee machine. Sometimes a secret rendezvous between two people in a closed "montage cabine" became the subject of amused gossip in the canteen.

Despite guardians at the main entrances, incidents unrelated to the main function of the building occurred. One might enter one of the dozens of small offices in the corridors to find a man seated at a well-equipped desk and later learn that he was completely unrelated with the work of the establishment and had simply found an empty office. When a group of workmen once removed a grand piano from one of the studios it was loaded on to a delivery vehicle parked outside the building. The instrument vanished without trace and no one knew who had organised the theft.

Of the various professions represented (journalists, maintenance and administrative personnel), the sound technicians surrounded by electronic equipment were the masters of their domain in their studios. Few would question their presence at all hours of the day and night. A technician invited me to join several speakers to record some stories for a producer of English language lessons to be sold in cassettes. Our employer made use of the studio facilities at night without authorisation and we worked into the small hours and were later privately paid for our services. To have reserved a commercial studio would have been prohibitively expensive.

News from and about the United States often imposed itself on the spectrum of world events. The assassination of President Kennedy in 1963 had already left its mark. In March, echoes of the on-going war in Vietnam coincided with signs of growing social unrest in France. Disturbances began in the suburban Nanterre University when six French students were detained after windows of several American banks and travel agencies in Paris had been shattered during anti-Vietnam war demonstrations. Four hundred students immediately began a sit-in strike to protest the arrest of their colleagues. A German-born student, Daniel Cohn-Bendit, promptly founded the 22nd March Movement and was later known as Danny the Red!

The French Existentialist philosopher, Jean-Paul Sartre, openly condemned the American military intervention in Vietnam with the words, "It is hard to recall a war with so little justification or such heroic resistance against overwhelming odds." His words were printed in a bilingual literary magazine published by an expatriate American bookseller in the Latin Quarter. George Whitman was to publish other poets and dissident intellectuals such as Marguerite Duras and Allen Ginsberg at his Shakespeare & Company bookshop. Visitors to Paris often stopped in front of the bookshop in the Latin Quarter out of curiosity to observe the decorative façade on the river-side facing Notre Dame cathedral. Originally a simple English language bookstore, it had developed into a meeting place for aspiring poets and writers. The Paris American Committee against the war met in the bookshop and Americans in France were invited to take part in demonstrations against the war in Viet Nam.

In the first week of April, the African-American Nobel Peace Prize winner Doctor Martin Luther King Junior was assassinated in Memphis, Tennessee. A champion of Civil Rights who had declared, "Injustice anywhere is a threat to justice everywhere," King had fought racial segregation and claimed political equality for his race with the memorable words in 1962, "My friends in Rocky Mount, I have a dream tonight...." I failed to turn up for duty on the night shift, Thursday the 4th of April, to announce the killing. As was the custom for a sudden absence in the studio, a colleague stepped in to replace me at the microphone. I, too, had had a dream and had overslept!

Our overseas radio service presented the world as seen from Paris but the growing political unrest in France could not be ignored among world news items we had broadcast. French opposition unions including the Communist Party and the left-wing Federation had joined the student movement with calls for social reforms in education, health-care, salaries and pensions. From April onwards, agitation had begun to spread to the provinces. Labour unions called for a general strike and a massive demonstration against the Gaullist government to coincide with the anniversary of the Fifth Republic. Prime Minister Georges Pompidou hastily returned from a visit to Afghanistan and publicly called for calm. The right-wing Gaullist regime was on the defensive.

1968 Student Revolt

The French student uprising began in earnest on the 14th of May in the western suburbs of Nanterre while an anarchist black flag was hoisted on the roof of the Sorbonne University in Paris. The Rector summoned the police to clear the university courtyard of a student meeting. The Sorbonne was evacuated by force and fifty-nine students were arrested. Riots spread through the Latin Quarter and many hundreds of students took to the streets. Trees and paving stones in the main avenues were uprooted to make barricades. The Odéon Theatre de France in the heart of the Latin Quarter was occupied by demonstrators and their supporters who painted slogans on its walls and safety-curtain. "Je suis marxist, tendance Groucho!" or "Il est interdit d'interdire." (It is forbidden to forbid.) The revolutionary action committee distributed leaflets headed, "Revolution is Dialogue," with invitations to take part in "dialogue with socially very different people." The incumbent actors Jean-Louis Barrault and Madeline Renaud took their places on the stage of the theatre to preside over public discussions about the growing crisis.

Widespread unrest swept the country, paralysing businesses and travel. The automobile factories of Renault, Peugeot and Citroen ceased production. There were calls for more objective reports from State radio and television services under the control of the Minister of Information.

Journalists of every branch of the media were invited by their respective trades unions to join a growing movement against State censorship. Students, the labour force and theatrical performers toured in procession around the outside of the radio station to alert the media.

Curious to observe the unrest in Paris that had become political French news, I left the office for the Latin Quarter and emerged from a Métro station to be assailed by clouds of tear-gas and a violent confrontation between CRS law forces and demonstrators. People were fleeing to avoid stones and sundry missiles hurled in the direction of uniformed police who were armed with shield and batons.

1968 French student riot poster;

Moving through streets strewn with debris, I joined a group of young people passing paving blocks from hand to hand to form a new barricade. French student unrest was echoed abroad. The British Beatles pop group caught the prevailing mood in France with Revolution, while the Rolling Stones echoed them with Street-Fighting Man.

President De Gaulle on a visit to French army headquarters in Baden-Baden, Germany to confer with General Massu, hastily returned to Paris to defend his leadership in a six-minute radio broadcast. He found the country deeply divided over the issues causing the unrest. He offered French citizens a choice between him and chaos, "between progress and upheaval," declaring "La reform, oui, la chienne en lit, non!" (Yes to reforms, but no to fouling the bed!)

As calm slowly returned to the capital after six weeks of nationwide disturbances, a pro-De Gaulle rally was announced. An estimated one thousand people had been injured in street fighting. The American correspondent of The New Yorker magazine, Janet Flanner, who signed herself Genêt, called the May disturbances, "the most unexpected and disastrous dozen days the country has known since the Commune of 1871." Her publisher warned her, "I don't want to know what you think.... I want to know what the French think." Jean-Louis Barrault and Madeline Renaud were dismissed from the State-run theatre they had worked in for more than ten years. The troublesome German-born student leader Daniel Cohn-Bendit, called Danny le Rouge, was expelled from France. The French philosopher Jean Paul Sartre remained faithful to the student's cause and openly questioned, "Who are their oppressors, if not the entire system of French society today?" The country meanwhile, awaited the outcome of a national referendum.

Back in our newsroom, I learned that the Soviet Union had launched Operation Danube. Tanks and troops of four of the five Warsaw Pact nations (East Germany, Poland, Hungary and Bulgaria) had invaded Czechoslovakia at twenty different points to converge on Prague in an attempt to crush the "Prague Springtime" movement of democratic socialism. Foreign Minister Jiri Hajek was forced to resign and Prime Minister Dubcek could offer no armed resistance to the invaders. The French Communist Party, which had earlier supported the invasion of Budapest, did not approve of the assault. A popular Czech singer Karel Cemoch, recorded a new song entitled, I Hope This Is Just A Bad Dream! A young Polish woman working in Prague decided to flee the unrest and make her way to France. With no money or travelling papers, she was soon to be at my doorstep on the Rue Cambronne.

Sunday afternoon, at the stroke of three at home, the world outside my window came to a shattering stop. A spluttering motor scooter split the air outside. Then silence, utter silence. For an awful moment, I too came to an empty full stop. Newspapers floated to the floor, legs and arms at all angles, I fell spinning to earth. As a child, I once had a book entitled Beyond the Blue Mountains by Clifford Mills. It was an allegory of life's adventures. It never told me of the detours one must make. As in a forest one loses sense of direction, my blue mountains now appeared only in the clouds above the rooftops. I closed my eyes and slept.

Once I carried my sack of prose across deserts like a guilty secret. Now Paris! City of asphalt, avenues of dust-encrusted mansions, grey cliffs of sculpted stone, not yet overgrown with an advancing jungle of glass and steel. That was why I liked the Rue de Rivoli with its long arcade selling souvenirs to tourists. Time was when I first visited France on a spring day half a century ago. Then the air crackled with talk and song; Boris Vian and Juliet Greco sang at Le Tabou in the Latin Quarter and Raymond Duncan left his Akadamia to stroll beside the Seine in flowing Greek toga and sandals. No longer. The world was heavy with earnestness and revolt, the colour of a Sunday supplement, raw, red, blurred. I know that I have arrived too late.

High summer beside the Seine in Paris. The sound of traffic is deadened below the blackened walls of the quais where summer visitors linger, stroll, sprawl beside the sluggish brown water. What am I waiting for? A miracle? I sit on steps half way down to the waters edge. Suddenly the traffic is stilled. One can clearly hear the sound of bamboo pipes being played across the Ile de la Cité. Deep below the depths of the city, a train rumbles by. The air-conditioned boats and barges go by with silent passengers watching the passing scene.

Every summer, it has been like this for years. They come in secret search and some find what they want. Tired words these from a tired man. That was why I was here. To try to recapture a certain freedom. To save myself. To begin again. Why? I don't know. Something has eluded me. Materially, I was finished. Morally compromised. (Maryse waited at home.) Could I survive my crisis? Could I begin to really live again? I felt that I was on the edge of a world of known and familiar things and values.

Chapter 4

Le plus ca change, plus c'est la meme chose.
(The more things change, the more they stay the same.)

Alphonse Karr (1808-1890) Les Guepes

THE FRENCH STATE RADIO and Television reflected the world in
words and images. News and information was the raw material
of all language services. Some items and events had greater import
than others but within the limits of time available, found their place
in scheduled programmes. A daily news flash in English on the French
national radio helped to keep summer visitors to France informed.
Meanwhile, the foreign radio service was expanding to include other
languages such as Mandarin.

As the world turned, the war in Viet Nam continued. President
Nixon sent American military forces into Cambodia (once part of
French Indo-China) without consulting Paris or London. While the
Viet Nam War peace talks continued in Versailles, France's State
Minister, André Malraux addressed an open letter to President Nixon
saying, "The USA has become the most powerful country on earth
without wanting to be.... That is why the U.S. makes war so well and
peace poorly." In the Middle East, Yasser Arafat became the leader
of the Palestine Liberation Organisation while Madame Golda Meir
became the head of the Israeli government in Jerusalem. In Prague,
a twenty-one year old Czech student of philosophy, Jan Palach, died
from self- immolation, protesting the Soviet invasion of his country.

In France, the Irish expatriate writer, Samuel Beckett, was awarded the Nobel Prize for Literature and the Franco-British supersonic Concorde aircraft first flew at Mach 1, the speed of sound.

On the domestic political front, President Charles De Gaulle left the capital for his home in Colombey-les-Deux-Eglises to vote as an ordinary citizen on the announced ten page referendum. When the country voted "Non" to the proposed future regional structure of the country and renovation of the Senate, De Gaulle penned a formal letter of resignation as President of the Fifth Republic. «Je cesse d'exercer mes fonctions de président de la République.» Within weeks, Georges Pompidou was elected President with Jacques Chaban-Delmas as his Prime Minister and Valery Giscard d'Estaing as Minister of Finance.

At home, we were now two sharing my modest living quarters in my hole in the sky; my real world was contained within four walls. Grazyna had fled the political upheaval in Prague after leaving her native Poland. We had met on the 14th of July, the French national holiday, in company with Olga and another friend. The four of us had sat at a café terrace near the Saint Michel fountain in the Latin Quarter. As we talked in a mixture of three languages, Grazyna's small face was alive with interest in the conversation although she spoke little or no French or English. My eyes darted from one to another, trying not to reveal too much interest in her whose native language I knew not one word. Later, we danced together at a traditional Fireman's Ball.

Our life together began walking through long grass at Versailles when the space between our hands shortened more quickly than a swallow's dive. When we stood up to leave, our cheeks were the colour of the sun touching the roofs of the Palace. Once we drove straight for the moon from the Paris Pont de Grenelle. "Keep straight on," she said as we sailed through the night. Another time, we sought a forest but in the end came out in flat country where a lighted factory hummed and clattered. We then knew we would not find what we had looked for that evening.

Our first task was to legalise her situation as a Polish immigrant. My new status as a journalist and our common address helped to overcome administrative obstacles. With the help of generous draughts of Stolichnaya (Russian vodka,) we finally officially joined three million inhabitants of Paris in their daily ritual of métro-boulot-dodo, a phrase coined by the French poet Pierre Béarn to mean "travel, work and sleep." I rarely knew if Grazyna was home sleeping or out exploring while I was at work. But in the evening, our two lives merged in laughter and tears as only Paris can offer two wanderers.

Grazyna's previous world was Slavic in culture. She had been a Polish television camerawoman who had also worked in Russia. She fully understood the fate of the protesting Prague student who had recently died from self-immolation. Now she sought a country where she could develop her artistic talents. While my time was mostly spent working on news at the office, my real world began when a pair of eyes fluttered beside me on a pillow as we jointly began to explore our personal hopes and fears.

Monday 21 July 1969. The Apollo 11 moon-shot was taking place. I was on the nightshift to present the dawn news bulletin. After months of "space-race" rivalry between the U.S. and the Soviets in the Cold War, three American astronauts were on board the spacecraft bound for a landing on the moon. Commander Neil Armstrong, with Mike Collins and Air Force Colonel Edwin "Buzz" Aldrin as crew, had been training for months for the ultimate test. The flickering images on our studio television screen was shared by millions around the world, as the Lunar Module "Eagle" landed in the dry dust of the Sea of Tranquillity.

At 3:56 hours French time, Neil Armstrong opened the hatch of the Lunar Module and cautiously took his first steps down to the surface of the moon. When we went on the air at dawn, it was the lead story of the morning bulletin. I repeated the words Neil Armstrong had spoken as he became the first man to set foot on the moon. "That's one small step for man, one giant leap for mankind." Armstrong had intended to say, "...one small step for A man," as an individual rather than speaking for humanity at large. Only later would the grammatical sense of his declaration be questioned, no less than when Edwin Aldrin planted the Star Spangled Banner in the dust of the moon's airless atmosphere. In the photo reproduced world-wide, was it really seen to be flapping in that windless moonscape? When one in five Americans disbelieved the image, NASA had to publicly refute that the flag episode had been recreated in the Nevada desert.

The drama we had watched all night seemed unreal and the poetic image of the moon had lost some of its magic. A once eternal symbol for poets and painters had become canalised by man. A triumph of applied mathematics in which the astronauts, for all their courage, were the passive subjects of a scientific experiment in remote control. In a single gesture, life and art had been joined.

Ah, Moon of my delight who know'st no wane,
The moon of Heav'n is rising once again:
How oft hereafter rising shall she look
Through this same garden after me – in vain!

Edward Fitzgerald (1809-1883)

Back across the river to my "Earth Module," I felt lifted out of temporary personal preoccupations. I had been one of the first to broadcast the landing on the moon, first to Africa and then in English on French national radio. After it was all over, I went into town and lunched in the Boulevard Saint-Germain while I watched the world go by. "How interesting people are in their diversity," I thought, "and how sad some of them appear." The drama we had watched all night seemed so unreal, yet it was the beginning of a new generation of super-men. Neil Armstrong gave almost no interviews about his adventure, while Edwin Aldrin gave lectures and later received aid for subsequent depression.

A short-wave listener and amateur astronomer in Virginia, USA, wrote, "Astronomy gives me great joy. Just being alone under the stars stretches my mind to its limits. Ever since I was a small child, the night sky fascinated me. I feel so very small and insignificant when I am under the night sky, yet I feel good that I can realize my place in the universe."

A radio station draws many creative people to its doors. Words and music are the raw material of the air waves and programmes in France tend to be multi-cultural for historical reasons. In our fifth-floor office, I was introduced to a young North African singer named Sapho. Born of a Jewish family in Marrakech, Morocco, Sapho's father was a singer in Arabic who had encouraged his daughter to express herself in song. As we sat in the studio for a recorded interview, Sapho giggled when I asked about her adopted name. It had nothing to do with the Sappho of

Greek mythology, she explained. For a new, unknown singer as she was, it was simply an original way to invite comment. Sapho writes poetry, designs and paints and sings in Spanish and had now decided to begin a new career in the City of Light.

Celebrated comedy duo, Stanley Laurel and Oliver Hardy

The first international celebrities I ever met were the film comedy duo, Laurel and Hardy. I had grown up with their cartoon images in children's magazines. A poster had announced they would perform in a north London music-hall as part of a tour at the end of their long careers. Doubting I would see the heroes of my youth in person but probably merely a couple of look-alikes, I travelled to the suburban township and sat through a mixed bill of comedy turns in a half empty hall, culminating in Stan and Ollie going through a familiar routine of bumping into each other when a wrong door was opened. Yes, it was my childhood heroes Stan Laurel and Oliver Hardy in the flesh!

After the show I waited alone in a dark corridor at a dimly-lit stage door until they reappeared from their dressing room. With an air of sadness, they shook my hand and actually thanked me for waiting to see them. If Oliver was huffy and impatient, Stan was gentle and kind to this adolescent and thanked me with a soft lilting voice for waiting to say hello to them. Then putting on their huge overcoats, they left the building and crossed a wide deserted pavement to where a dusty Rolls Royce was waiting and disappeared into the London fog. The glow of recognition and the awareness of a certain sadness behind the laughter and applause have stayed with me. It was my first lesson in the innate modesty of established great performers.

My new job in France offered me the opportunity of meeting confirmed theatrical personalities. France's "Grand Old Man of Song," Maurice Chevalier, had just given his last solo concert at the Champs Elysees Theatre and was about to publish yet another book of his memoirs entitled, I Remember It Well. I decided to seek an interview with the eighty-three year old veteran now living in semi-retirement outside Paris. A call to his secretary and I was given an appointment at his home in the village of Marnes-la-Coquette. His private estate lay bordering a secluded country lane in a village still beyond the reach of auto routes and new suburban townships. As I drove out of the capital to meet the archetype French boulevardier, smiling and confident in innumerable public appearances, I wondered if Maurice Chevalier was really like that in real life.

While I waited in the car for the appointed hour, a limousine bearing an American number plate drew up near me and heads craned from the windows to stare at the elegant white-painted mansion of La Louque, named after his mother. Then the visitors raced away, another French monument dutifully ticked off by pilgrims from the west. It was Chevalier's singing of the unforgettable Louise in his first Hollywood film, The Innocents of Paris, in 1929 that had launched him internationally.

Chevalier at Home

At half past the hour, I crossed the road and rang the bell and stepped into the past. Sunlit gardens stretched away beyond an entrance-hall crowded with mementoes: a portrait of his mother and inevitably, a straw hat set at an angle on a hatter's dummy. I was shown into a large sitting room. Precisely on cue, Maurice appeared down an internal staircase, short blue housecoat, red slacks, small feet in slippers, silver hair neatly brushed and parted and pink cheeks glowing, a picture of comfortable good health. We shook hands and he sat beside me on a couch while his secretary observed yet another interview with the man whose image and voice were known to millions. He appeared completely at ease as we chatted in English while my tape recorder turned silently at our feet.

Maurice Chevalier, veteran French singer.

"Maurice Chevalier, in your eighty-third year, how do you view life in general after your long years of effort?"

"When you've known the world that I have known, after singing for sixty-eight years, I cannot see the world of today with great enthusiasm," he said simply.

I searched his face as he was talking; unlined features, small nose, effortless diction.

"You have been quoted as saying, 'Old age is not so bad when you consider the alternative.' What about the alternative, Maurice Chevalier?"

I had in mind his words that he used to be "the oldest of the young and now he had become the youngest of the old." He stared at me as he composed his reply.

"The alternative is becoming something very ordinary. People die by the thousands everywhere, so even death is not so important as it used to be."

In common with other celebrities, I remembered that he had had great difficulty in accepting the loneliness of his retirement.

"Is there anything you haven't done in your life that you still want to do?" I asked.

"No, I think I've done the very best I could do with what I knew how to do. My last tour of England three years ago has been a wonderful experience because my last show was at the London Palladium, and I've been very proud to see a difficult audience like that standing up from the stalls to the gallery.... Even in the English provinces I've been very touched; it seemed to me I went stronger in the English provinces than at any time in my career. That is a great memory for me. You know, I am having an eternal love affair with the public. When I see the audience standing and clapping, for me it is my tonic!"

I recalled the unhappy time when he was banned from making a tour of England after his performances before German occupying forces in France during the war. He later publicly justified his appearances by saying, "An entertainer's profession is his whole life. If we have to fight for France or die for her, we are ready to do so. But for the rest of the time, we just want to be left alone. I guess we feel we are doing our share by giving laughter and gaiety to the nation." He was later reported to have donated money to the Resistance "maquis" forces of the Perigord region. He was not the only French theatrical celebrity to have defended his profession during that troubled period of French history. He had served as a soldier in the First World War and had escaped on foot with a fellow prisoner from a German Stalag war camp.

He stood waving a friendly "Au revoir!" at his front door as I drove away. It was my first and only meeting with him, but not the last time I watched him in action. He was driven in an open car through the

Tuileries Gardens a few weeks later during a public event, waving to the admiring crowds like a monarch. I was mildly surprised at the lack of interest when I presented my exclusive interview to my journalist colleagues.

In a pause from editing the news each day, I decided to record some atmospheric sound for a radio feature on the church bells of Paris. The project had begun with a visit to the southern bell-tower of Notre Dame Cathedral where I had laid my hand on the colossal 13,000 kilo Marie-Thérèse bourdon bell. Since the Revolution, Paris still possessed a hundred bell-towers despite many bronze bells having been melted to make cannons. In the Church of Saint-Germain l'Auxerrois next to the Louvre museum, I learned that mechanical tolling had replaced the traditional bell-ringers in many French churches.

I took my tape recorder to Montmartre and sat opposite the church of Saint-Jean at Abbesse waiting for a service to end. It was cold. No bells sounded. Down in the Rue Lepic, a busy shopping street leading from the Place Blanche, I heard a familiar voice and saw a slender female figure in slacks walking among the shoppers singing "Quand nous chanterons le temps des cerises...." Catherine Sauvage was singing to an invisible recorded orchestra for a film about Montmartre. As she continued to stroll within camera range, local trades people called out, "Look, there's Catherine! Salut Catherine! Ca va?" Pretending not to hear their greeting, she continued to sing the classic song of the Commune of 1871.

J'aimerai toujours le temps des cerises
C'est de ce temps-là que je garde au cœur
Une plaie ouverte
Et Dame Fortune, en m'étant offerte
Ne saura jamais calmer ma douleur
J'aimerai toujours le temps des cerises
Et le souvenir que je garde au cœur.

Cherry Blossom Time was written by Jean-Baptiste Clément and A. Renard in 1867. Doubtless the Austrian film producers knew its history. Presenting myself as journalist, Madame Sauvage kindly invited me to her home outside the capital. She made no secret of her need to improve her English in conversation with me!

Chapter 5

"The old Paris is no more. The shape of a city changes more quickly, alas, than the heart of a mortal."

Charles Baudelaire, Le Cygne (Les Fleurs du Mal, 1861)

THE DECADE OF THE Sixties ended with the tolling of bells when President Charles de Gaulle died at his country home in Colombey-les-Deux Eglises. On a sunny afternoon in November, women and children in the gardens surrounding Notre Dame Cathedral looked up when the bell-ringers began to toll the great thirteen ton bourdon bell. Leaders of more than eighty nations stood shoulder to shoulder in the nave of the cathedral to pay homage to the man who had saved France in her hour of need. Newly elected President Georges Pompidou publicly announced "France is a widow!"

The world was changing at an ever increasing rate. Some of the values that belonged to France's Fifth Republic now seemed in need of re-examination. The old order had begun to change in 1968 when many of the earlier institutions and traditions continued to defend their existence. By virtue of its geographical position, France had given Europe and the world unrivalled culture, art and a tradition of gracious living. But in a unified and peaceful Europe, it lacked the bargaining counter of natural energy sources and political leadership. Economically, France was no longer the centre of the western world.

The seventies began a period of anguish for Paris. The city was being torn apart by renovation and building projects. The skyline was topped by giant tower-cranes swinging silently above gangs of workmen handling building materials. With an estimated nine and a half million inhabitants in the greater Paris region, the capital was the fourth largest agglomerate after Tokyo, London and New York. After several years of tunnelling, new fast Métro lines were nearing completion to serve suburban town centres. The silhouette of concrete fingers pointing skyward was already visible west of the capital where a new business quarter, La Défense was emerging, named after the defence of Paris during the Franco-Prussian war. It was the beginning of a quarter later to be dubbed "Little Manhattan."

A Paris Métro tunnel in the western suburb.

Wearing the obligatory safety helmet to interview construction workers I walked westward in a new underground Métro tunnel before the first trains began their four-minute trip from central Paris to La Défense. I then climbed to the summit of the new Nobel Tower on the banks of Seine and stood with a smart-suited businessman looking back at roofs and spires of traditional Paris. A dark finger of stone was emerging in the heart of the Montparnasse quarter where the erecting of a 660 foot tall office building had begun. The characterless tower block standing alone, said to be the tallest in Europe, was to disfigure and transform the historic artistic quarter of Left Bank Paris. It was the innovative Swiss architect Charles-Edouard Jenneret, known as Le Corbusier, who had suggested that verticality was the solution to the problem of space in Paris.

Studio 130, 6:30 am.

"Good Morning! This is the ORTF, the French Broadcasting System, coming to you from Paris. Due to a strike of sound technicians, our news bulletin this morning will be of short duration and contain only today's main news headlines.

"President Nixon has announced the end of conflict in North Vietnam.

Denmark, Britain and Ireland are officially to join the European Economic Community.

Twenty-one people on board a military aircraft were killed when their plane crashed in the centre of France. The passengers, members of the French Atomic Agency Commission, included two Generals and an Admiral."

There followed a musical interlude.

"Headline news in the French press announced the death of Maurice Chevalier."

'France's grand old man of song' had died at his home in Marne-la-Coquette. His life and work was extensively reviewed by the media. My recent interview at his home was suddenly in demand for memorial programmes from our service.

The veteran French film director, René Clair, offered his tribute to Maurice Chevalier in the daily Le Figaro, and quoted the entertainer asking humorously, "What lucky star allowed me to sing without a voice for almost half a century?" René Clair remarked, "He created a style of his own with a wink of complicity, childish charm and friendly good nature, and kept it without taking it seriously." Chevalier had indeed always shamelessly exploited his rich French accent in English films and songs. The working-class boy had come a long way from the Ménilmontant quarter of Paris where he had first sang for centimes in bars at the age of ten. On the day of his funeral, I joined a large crowd of mourners at his tomb in the village cemetery and paid homage to him in the traditional Catholic manner.

At his fourth press conference in Paris, President Pompidou reviewed the future and announced that he was visiting Africa again "in the spirit of continuity of the work of General de Gaulle." On the home front, he said he was pursuing the main lines of reforms begun by his predecessor. Mr. Pompidou also dealt with his conception of the construction of Europe, of the creation of an integrated European economy and the possibility of a future confederation of states administered by a European Government with a European Parliament.

In response to recent calls for more objective reporting by the French media, Pompidou remarked, "News should not be deflected from its true meaning. French television and national radio should be truly impartial and worthy of our country, of which they are and should be, the expression." Such a declaration from a head of state who had once been a specialist in literature at university and editor of an anthology of poetry, augured well for the future of French journalism. Other reforms were already underway to offer greater freedom of opinion. Paid advertising was to appear for the first time on French State television.

Central Africa

Then came the day I was chosen to join a team of French and foreign journalists to accompany President Pompidou on an official State visit to Niger and Chad, two former colonies in French Equatorial Africa. France had been the biggest colonialist on the African continent after Portugal. The dissolution of the former French Empire in Africa had almost ended by 1960. Zaire had already gained its independence from Belgium in 1960 and Rhodesia had become a Republic in 1970. France had relinquished all its African possessions (except Algeria) during the years of the Fifth Republic. Racial conflicts involving capitalist and socialist forces had sometimes become the legacy of the colonial epoch. Portugal's recent withdrawal from Angola had already sparked a civil war.

Half of all African countries are English-speaking. Among the hundreds of local dialects in use, the French language had remained an element of national unity in both the Niger and Chad Republics. Radio offered the most direct means of addressing former colonies. France had established two radio transmitting stations in Gabon and the Congo-Brazzaville and a third was planned in Guyana, Latin America. The vast potential listenership often had little access to the printed press and was dependent on indigenous local languages for their news and information.

Rapid research in the archives informed me that most of the four million inhabitants of the Niger Republic were farmers belonging to either the Hausa or Fulani tribes. But only three per cent of their vast land south of the Sahara was cultivated. French was taught in Niger schools and President Dior Hamani claimed that his ambition was to serve as a liaison between black and white Africa. The French Presidential visit to Niger was not unrelated to the discovery by the French Atomic Energy Commission of a valuable natural resource, uranium at Arlit, some 500 miles from the capital, Niamey.

The adjacent Chad Republic, the largest of four land-locked Equatorial African countries had three and a half million inhabitants. An Islamic country since the 18th century, whose main product is cotton, Chad was the first French colony to rally to De Gaulle and the Free French forces in the war in 1944. But independence had produced a power struggle among the superpowers for raw materials coupled with financial aid. While the influence of France and Great Britain had declined, the roles of the Soviet Union and the United States of America as nuclear superpowers increased, the problem of apartheid, or racial segregation in distant South Africa, remained an unsettling problem.

Our Presidential mission was preceded by a briefing and inoculations against yellow fever and malaria, deadly diseases that annually kill a million Africans. Dark suits and bow ties were needed for the official receptions in the two capitals. It was only when I and some thirty colleague journalists were flying for five hours across the desert wastes of the Sahara, the world's second largest desert nearly the size of the United States, that I realized the scale of the African continent. The landlocked Niger and Chad Republics are each twice the area of France and are entirely surrounded by some forty other African states. The area of the entire continent could easily accommodate the USA, Europe and India together, with still more space to fill. A veteran journalist of African missions regaled us during the flight with stories of early western missionaries to Africa. "First, they offered them Bibles and invited them to pray. And when they opened their eyes, they had the Bibles in their hands and we had their land!"

Our mission followed a well-established ritual. Huge crowds greeted our arrival at Niamey airport, waving at President Pompidou standing in an open car next to President Diori Hamani. We followed in open vehicles while African students demonstrated for more French aid to coincide with their annual Tabaski Moslem holiday. The official programme included a private lunch for President Pompidou and his wife at the Presidential palace. Later, Mr. Pompidou addressed the Niger National Assembly and gave a press conference. Our reception by President Francois Tombalbaye in the Chad capital of Fort Lamy followed a similar programme. In his declarations, the French President pursued the Gaullist doctrine of cooperation between the developed and developing nations, never publicly using the phrase "under-developed nations."

The strong journalistic presence gave the visits to both African capitals an air of importance. The Presidents congratulated one another for the friendly relations between their two countries and France. Prepared texts were available of the speeches and the assembly was invited to meet informally with refreshments during which we were able to observe President Pompidou and his wife at close quarters. There was no hint of an impending health problem for the French head of state as he sat quietly observing the assembly. It all seemed like a familiar Parisian gathering with each journalist recording his impressions, except that we were in a land several thousand miles from Europe of which most of us had never previously given a thought.

As we flew northward back across the Sahara, I reflected that I had barely scratched the surface of an unknown world and had not even had a moment's intimate conversation with an African man or woman or a member of the race of Tuaregs. Neither had there been time to see the Niger national park with its fauna and flora or even the great Niger "djoliba" river and Lake Chad, whose level is constantly threatened by the encroaching Sahara desert. I resolved to read André Gide's Retour du Tchad on my return to Paris and turned my thoughts to home and how Grazyna had been spending the days of my absence.

On arrival home, Grazyna presented me with Kuska, a cat she had rescued entangled in a tennis net in the school grounds near our house. She was afraid I would say no to the new arrival and announced, "Now we are four!" a joking reference to Michau, her teddy bear. Kuska disappeared a few weeks later, but not before I had risked my life trying to rescue the animal from our rooftop. Grazyna announced that she was going to visit the island of Corsica (with Michau) to do some painting. I returned to my daily routine of presenting the news and researching new material for announced feature programmes to augment our daily output.

In the daily flood of news items, anecdotes about contemporary life sometimes offered light relief. We could overlook a news flash from New Zealand general elections where a candidate registered himself as Mr. Mickey Mouse or a bill before the Australian parliament to ban the words "dago" and "wog" to ease race relations. On the home ground, a 35 year-old French house-painter tried to drive his car under the Arc de Triomphe. To the disbelief of the guard of the monument at the head of the Champs Elysées Avenue, he had unhooked the chains protecting the Tomb of the Unknown Soldier. He was immediately arrested and sentenced to one month in prison for attempted desecration of a sacred site while under the influence of alcohol.

Still on home ground, a pilot of a light aircraft from Basel, Switzerland circled over the Paris region (called the Ile de France) and made a perfect landing on Runway Number One at Roissy airport. When the pilot looked around the deserted runway, no airport official came to greet him. He had landed at the new Roissy-France airport, not due to open until March 1974. He had mistaken it for the older Le Bourget airport south of the capital!

The former Paris central food market Les Halles had moved to the southern suburb of Rungis, near the Orly international airport. The evacuation of the old market had provoked waves of emotion from traders whose families had worked there for generations. My spontaneous eyewitness account of protest demonstrations in the heart of the French capital was broadcast on Radio 4 from the BBC in London. While property developers continued to draft plans to exploit the huge potentially vacant site, the vast empty halls and underground store-rooms had been occupied by itinerant performers and musicians.

Among the numerous artists and musicians using the abandoned pavilions, I found a young guitarist performing his own compositions. Seventeen year old Daniel Guichard, whose family had grown up in the quarter, sang of watching part of his childhood disappear with the theme "The stomach of Paris has gone but not its heart." His inspirations would later carry him to national celebrity. Back at the news desk, I learned that another American Apollo space mission to the moon was streaking back to earth at twelve kilometres a second, while simultaneously the ruins of Baltard Pavilion No. 11 in central Paris, fell to the ground in a cloud of debris during demolition.

The early Balthard central Paris food market.

Plans to adopt and re-erect the historic iron and glass pavilions were examined by the Paris municipal authorities but costs deterred would-be buyers. The Mayor of suburban Nogent on the River Marne offered to re-erect pavilion No. 8 for his Commune saying that it would become a cultural and artistic exhibition hall. He then announced that the historic electric organ from the huge Paris Gaumont Palace cinema, formerly L'Hippodrome, had been bought at auction for 200,000 francs and would be installed in the newly erected Baltard pavilion. The organ, capable of producing special sound effects to accompany silent films, was listed as an historic instrument that could not legally leave French territory or be destroyed. The market pavilion that had once housed poultry would now resound to electronic organ music.

Short-wave radio transmissions had its mysteries, known only to sound specialists, as the Reuters news agency reported from the U.S. Listener George Dillard, in New York, was having problems with his new false teeth. They kept him awake at night relaying music that no one else in his room could hear. Experts who were consulted said that the metal in his teeth "defected" the station signal from a Connecticut radio station and his jawbone amplified it. He now takes his teeth out at night and sleeps better without them, the Reuters report added.

One morning, I had the strangest sensation when I drew aside the curtain which covers my single window. A bright facade of sunlit buildings stared back at me with threatening clarity. Our house overlooked a wide area of old two-storey buildings and a vacant area where houses had been demolished, leaving rubble and a fragment of a wall with a single house number still visible. Beyond that plot, where children and cats played, there were soaring new blocks of flats, brash clean lines of concrete, still empty of inhabitants. I stared disbelieving as these structures stared back at me, menacingly, aggressively.

A visiting journalist from Radio Ghana was not slow to notice the changing face of Paris. He wrote to us, "The wonderful and beautiful city which is being destroyed by those who think they are helping to solve the housing problem. I wish I could convince them to stop their mad business," signed J.V.Kumapley.

With growing listenership in African countries and transmitters in the Congo-Brazzaville, African local correspondents began to contribute to our programmes and African trainees joined our team in Paris. They brought with them intimate knowledge of their country and culture. While some newcomers to France imagined that life was easy in Paris, they quickly learned that hard work and discipline were required to integrate into the life of the capital. A note left on my desk by an African "staigaire" or trainee, read thus: "I'm hungry and must eat. So I'm going to request the cashier at the cafeteria self-service to debit your section. I'm sure you'd not wish to see me starve in spite of other things." It was signed by Ted Oke.

Now it comes again, that great empty middle of the afternoon, seeping in at the half-open window. I hear the city give a great gasp and a sigh, as though from exhaustion or despair and I see myself transfixed in the centre of the room, unable to move one way the other, helpless to use my brain or to take a single, simple decision to move from the window to the door.

Chapter 6

"The ole days are gone forever
And the new ones ain't far behind."

Bob Dylan

ODAY IN PARIS, THE rain sweeps down on my single potted geranium outside the door. It stands on an ornate white chair that Grazyna rescued from discarded rubbish in the Rue Sablonnière, where the donkeys are stabled. The chair and the plant, standing in the rain, the folded Sunday newspaper in my lap, begin to form a pattern in my mind, of something found, something lost, something past, something forgotten. How gratifying to read Raymond Mortimer (whom I once visited) writing on Walter Sickert who died in 1942. I can still remember the atmosphere of the London Sickert painted with such restraint. And the musty corridors of Collins Music Hall, with its sad comics staring out at the empty seats and dozing customers. A dying vestige of a London I hardly knew but sensed in my nostrils when as an adolescent I wandered through the streets on a Sunday.

With my regular job at the French radio station, I was living simultaneously in two separate worlds, the past and the present. At home, my past is omnipresent. Music and memories and pages of notes recall the people and events that have shaped me. A page of excursions to Paris, Rome, Cairo, Istanbul…. I was there! I left my heart in a hundred cities, towns and villages but it remains intact, giving new thrills of anticipation but also fear of failure. I hold the pieces in my hand, fragments drawn or torn, from contexts as varied as time will allow. How can I bring together the strings of so many places and people to a coherent conclusion?

Reactions to world events were often reflected in letters we received from listeners in distant countries. Mr. Jacques Fis in the Yesilkoy suburb of Istanbul, Turkey, wrote, "I am always well-informed about French affairs. Well, it's all very much the same as it has been for years; strikes, protests, workers wages, demands, counter demands, and overlying all that, the perennial struggle for power. A struggle which is just as perennial in Turkey as it is in France.... The funny game of politics. The game of life is not so funny, when reality appears to us in all its nakedness."

Our listener's observation of political leadership was confirmed with the news that Turkish troops had invaded the northern shores of the island of Cyprus, protesting against the possible union of Cyprus with Greece. Turkish forces had reached the eastern port of Famagusta to consolidate their presence in the north and joined forces with Turkish Cypriots. Several thousand Greeks fled Famagusta in a convoy when the invading forces used high explosives in bomb attacks. The Cypriot President Glafkos Clerides has called on Greek Cypriots to "fight to the last drop of Greek blood" against any build-up of the new Turkish presence. An administrative Green Line separating the opposing forces was established and UN peacekeeping forces strengthened. Aphrodite's Island of Love was now rent with upheaval and conflict that would involve the emerging European community of nations and the United Nations organisation.

A dawn news programme with Marie-Claude. Pleasant company, effortless broadcast. Another one away! We file and leave the building. I take my car to Boulogne-Billancourt and find a garage to change my number plates, then sit in the sun with a beer as the morning progresses. Lunch in a Breton restaurant. The pretty young daughter of the house serves me. When she smiles, there's a gap where some teeth are missing. On the walls, some Breton traditional costumes and pictures by the celebrated photographer, Raymond Depardon, who had filmed and photographed General de Gaulle.

Home tired and thoughtful. Then to the cinema museum at Chaillot Palace to see the Luis Buñuel film Les Hauts de Hurlevent (Wuthering

Heights.) Like a TV film with Wagner's music! Outside the cinema, the evening sky was rosily coloured and delicate. I had the momentary feeling of supreme contentment as I gazed across the Paris skyline. I thought of Grazyna painting in Corsica. Below the Palace, the river Seine flowed imperturbably under the bridges, a reminder that nature had its ways of keeping a balance between the past and the present.

At home, I tried to read some of André Malraux's Anti-Memoirs though I feel I don't like him very much. As Minister of Culture during the student uprising in 1968, he had sacked André Langlois, the creator of the cinema museum in 1963 and conservator of old forgotten films. Langlois was relieved of his job because of allegedly poor management of the state-funded museum. Rumour had it that the cans of old films he acquired were poorly stored at home in his bathtub. Langlois publicly recalled that France was a country of motion picture pioneers. Following protests by an appreciative public, he was reinstated as the director of the Paris cinema museum which included a collection of old cameras, projectors and costumes. Langlois knew and respected the cinema and its public who were sure that advertised films of their choice would be presented exactly on time without commercial advertising or announcements of forthcoming features.

Radio journalists often receive offers to work for other media; translations, film sub-titles and even independent commentaries. The scope was wide but privileges and existing contractual obligations had to be respected. Thus, when I was invited to contribute a regular feature for the Australian Broadcasting Commission, I briefly adopted a new identity on the air. I was torn between two points of view; to subscribe to the traditional images of Paris and France, for those who may never have visited the country, or to tell the truth as it appears to a newcomer like myself. Given freedom of subject, I opted to alternate between the two attitudes in succeeding features. Paris was not only the world's most visited tourist capital with its images of the Eiffel Tower, Le Moulin Rouge, fashion and good food and wine but was also a city constantly suffering from growing pains and development coupled with political unrest.

The Sounds of Paris

When I hauled my heavy Nagra recording machine into the streets, it was to illustrate a city in torment struggling to adapt to changing times while trying to retain a past of architectural elegance. Creating a radio feature is like cooking; the ingredients are words and sounds which combine to produce a final message within a given time limit. Sounds and voices play an evocative role. The cries of a homeless beggar, police sirens, the shouts of vendors in street markets, the endless chatter of crowds in shops and restaurants, the sound of birdsongs at dusk or the lilting melodies of a Barbery organ, all add to the atmosphere for the final editing of a feature.

To continue my search for the sounds of the city, I lugged my heavy tape recorder on my shoulder to Place de L'Opera, with the idea of getting some atmospheric noise of traffic, police whistles, tourists…. But it was cold, people were sheltering in cafés and I was tired after reading the news at dawn. When I finally found a policeman blowing his whistle at the Palais Royale, the volume needle of the machine refused to register any response. I cursed all machines and returned home to my tiny cupboard in the 15th district.

The French press reported a growing crisis at the historic Jardin des Plantes of the Natural History Museum in Paris. The gardens and menagerie on the banks of the Seine, reputedly the world's oldest zoological gardens, were in financial trouble. For more than a century, African birds and beasts have lived in cages for the pleasure of Parisians, the general public and to the surprise of passing visitors. Gone were the days when an orangutan once sat at a table with its keeper and ate with a spoon or an elephant swayed to the rhythm of a live orchestra before falling asleep during a symphony. The ministries responsible were being called upon to renovate the zoo and save the remaining livestock of birds, mammals and fish from extinction.

I took a lonely walk through the gardens. Caged animals paced behind bars or stood staring at visitors. All appeared sad and abandoned in the middle of dusty, grey Paris. I asked to see the person responsible for the animals and was introduced to Madame M and Professor Jacques Nouvel. We talked about how old and charming the quarter is, a veritable museum of architectural styles. A white-coated zoologist came into the room and whispered, "It's still alive!" I silently wondered to what animal he referred. Madame M then offers me some colour slides for our up-coming summer television newscasts for visitors. I thanked them for their time and trouble.

Freelance work

Blandine was a petite Parisienne with large soulful eyes and hair drawn back in a pony-tail. She looked like a high-school student but was in fact a young business woman handling television documentary films for export abroad which involved any one of three systems of translation from French into English. The simplest method was sub-titling on the film, or the sound can be suppressed for "voice-over" recording or the more difficult and expensive "lip-sync" dubbing with actors. Whatever system used, a certain knowledge or familiarity with English is required. Already used to the demands of sound recording, I briefly became her assistant for whatever work was needed to serve the flow of films for the English-speaking market abroad.

Among the offers of occasional work for English speakers, I was recruited to take part in a new sound recording of Abel Gance's classic silent film, Napoléon Bonaparte. It was a joint participation by a group of actors to re-record a sound version of the 1926 film, already reworked in 1934 for projection on three screens simultaneously in anticipation of wide-screen and cinemascope presentation.

Abel Gance was the archetype film-maker, experimenter, poet, with an epic vision, willing to put his hand to the smallest mechanical detail of film-making. He had even tried filming parts of Napoléon in relief. Like many other pioneers he was caught between the silent screen and the advent of sound film. Napoléon Bonaparte was first shot silent at the moment when Al Jolson first opened his mouth in a commercial sound film, The Jazz Singer in 1927. But Gance had his own way of telling a story in film. Who else would have hurled a camera into the air with the motor running to simulate what the world looked like from a swooping bird, or strapped a camera on the back of a horse to record the jogging motion? Still active in his late seventies, Gance had presided over the French Spring Film Festival at Hyères in 1967.

Out to the CIS studios in the western suburb of Courbevoie to join a crew of dubbing actors for a sound version of Bonaparte. I met the other speakers in the parking lot before entering the studio to meet

Abel Gance and the sound technicians. Then the screen come alive with images. We watched brief fragments of the original film projected on a huge screen. Then we were told our roles. The usual long pauses for technical reasons. We were issued with the music score and words of Onward Christian Soldiers to sing. Between takes, we watched Abel Gance striding back and forth below the huge screen, hands behind his back, ruminating about the work. Came our turn to provide the sounds of soldiers. We strode in a circle under a microphone and rehearsed the singing of marching columns. I was later able to give the required cry of anguish as a gun carriage ran over the legs of a screen actor lying wounded on the battlefield. We all felt we had been at war under the command of Emperor Gance but hardly got a glimpse of Albert Dieudonné who played the role of Napoléon on the screen. History had briefly come alive. Then we returned to reality.

Back in the office, I learned that a celebrated African-American entertainer was in the news for her personal problems and outspokenness. As an established music-hall artiste, Josephine Baker's name occurred frequently in the news, not only in relation to her profession but concerning her private life. Since her leap to fame in the Twenties, she had made France her home but was in financial trouble trying to maintain a family of twelve orphans in her medieval château in southwest France. Costs were mounting, hence her recent appearances in London and New York to try to pay off debts. Josephine Baker's long struggle to continue to sing and dance, while openly proclaiming her anti-racial stance, was the frequent subject of discussion in France. Fellow performers and admirers, notably the French screen actress, Brigitte Bardot, were rallying to her support with appeals for funds on television. I resolved to find out more about this black artiste.

Home after midnight following a Sarah Vaughan concert at the Paris Palais des Sports arena. Not the best evening for her. A cool audience of more than three thousand. Sarah nearly collapsed from tiredness in full view and had to take the pianists seat on the stage. Later in her dressing-room to meet the press, she passed around a bottle of whisky. There followed embarrassing foolish conversations. Thanking her, we sadly left for our offices and homes.

Today's midday programme passed with fumbled delivery of some items. Then we broadcast my feature on the tri-centenary of the death of the French dramatist, Jean-Baptiste Molière. The recording was in good hands. Gerald, the producer, knew his job and did not mangle my script or choice of music and interview extracts. Molière was a master of satire, ridiculing conventional behaviour during the time of King Louis XIV. One of his best known plays, Le Malade Imaginaire was born of his own mortal illness. "Most men die, not of their diseases, but of their remedies," he wrote. What would Molière say of today's France's generous medical services and abundance of medicines and concern with the nation's health? The documentalist at the Molière archives at the Comedie Française, the French National Repertory Theatre, reminded me that Molière left no working notes of manuscripts and little is known of his private life. If the age of the Sun King seems remote to us today, the day-to-day life of 17th century France appears vivid and alive in his comedies. He then reminded me that the language of Molière was the equivalent in France of the English of Shakespeare.

Off to the TV studio near the Champs Elysées for colour tests for our summer series of newscasts for English-speaking visitors to France. Patient cameramen and a producer were listening to readings of specimen bulletins. Appalled by my worried look and my lopsided face and thin-lipped grimace in the replays, I was advised to relax and allow for facial animation and humour. We go on French national television in July. Another step in the great adventure. Another first! It must be good!

The morning was spent in the Bois de Boulogne with Elizabeth during the filming of a feature starring Marcello Mastroianni. Yves Robert, the director conferred with his team. The sun not yet through the clouds, the mist still rising from the lake. I watched some charming scenes with Francoise Fabien and Mastroianni meeting, embracing and then getting into a boat to take them to the island restaurant. During a pause in filming, Mastroianni walked with me through the trees and we chatted in French about how he likes being in Paris. His first international success had been in "Paris est toujours Paris" in 1951. Elizabeth and I later lunched with the film crew on the island.

In the evening, I attended a concert featuring Duke Ellington in the Palais des Sports. The huge hall was full of admirers of the visiting celebrity. At the beginning, the Duke called out asking if his musician friend, Claude Bolling was present. The recital then proceeded to acclaim. The audience was dutifully stilled when the Duke played his closing piano solo. The evening ended with a standing ovation. As I waited backstage with other journalists to greet the performer, we became aware that he was under physical stress. Two assistants helped him up the stairs to his waiting car. I exchanged a few words with him as he took his seat. After his Paris appearance, I was aware that it might well be his last visit to France. The Duke could not have remembered our earlier meeting at the Winter Gardens concert-hall in the English coastal town of Bournemouth a few years earlier. Here in Paris, I had been privileged to again meet the musician and composer whose achievements were already part of entertainment history.

Death of a President

In April 1974, Georges Pompidou suddenly died at his home in Paris. At sixty-four, he was the first French President to have served only five years of his elected seven-year term. Discretely known to be suffering from an unnamed illness, his bloated facial appearance had revealed medication to combat cancer. Despite his chronic illness, he had visited Russia and China the previous year. I recalled his modest demeanour at receptions when seated with his wife during his official visits to central Africa but taking little active part in the festivities.

Six days after the death of Georges Pompidou, forty-eight year old Valery Giscard d'Estaing officially announced his candidacy for the Presidency. The son of a Deputy and a former provincial Mayor, Giscard d'Estaing, was an economist and Centre Right Liberal who liked to impart his own view of life. During a brief Presidential election campaign he joined a football team, dined with senior citizens in their home and even played the accordion in public. Within a few months, he was elected the 20th President of the Republic by a narrow margin of votes against the Socialist rival, Francois Mitterrand.

On the evening of the official election results, I joined journalists and supporters at the Independent Republican campaign headquarters. Taking my turn with French-speaking colleagues, I thrust my microphone forward and asked the newly elected President of the Fifth French Republic to say a few words for our English-speaking listeners. Without hesitation, he spoke of his gratitude to the French electorate for their confidence in him. It was an innovation for a French leader to address the media in English. Most are afraid of making errors and later misinterpretation and prefer to rely on translation.

Back in our offices my colleagues were delighted when we aired the new French President's statement in our English service. The defence of the language of Molière has always been a principle of French public utterances. With a few well chosen words, Giscard later astonished millions of French citizens in a television address, saying in English, "My role is not to please but to serve France!"

The Paris newspaper "La Croix" immediately noted that the new French President addressed the English media in a way that went beyond mere public relations and signified an exceptional development for France. The paper even joked that such a development risks making obsolete the English-language service of the foreign language radio service. The new President quickly became informally known as VGE in all the media. Raymond Depardon discretely filmed electoral campaign would mysteriously remain unseen by the public for nearly thirty years.

Josephine Baker

The American performer, Josephine Baker, who had made France her home, was in the news again. She had lost her chateau due to serious debts and had moved to Monaco with her family of adopted children, thanks to the intervention of Princess Grace who was the President of the Monaco Red Cross Association. Baker's appearances in Monte Carlo had produced offers of a return to Paris for an appearance on the 50th anniversary of her arrival in France in 1925. Preparations were already ahead in Paris for the opening of "Joséphine" at the neighbourhood Bobino Theatre in Montparnasse. The "rags-to-riches" story of the black girl who brought the Charleston dance to Europe had all the ingredients to please sophisticated Paris audiences.

American entertainer Josephine Baker flying to London in 1933.

The Bobino Theatre had a long history of popular entertainment when Montparnasse was once situated in a rural Paris suburb. On a narrow street called the Rue de la Gaîté, I pushed open an unmarked door at the back of the theatre and came face-to-face with Josephine Baker, sitting on an upright wooden chair singing to a tape recorder with a music stand in front of her. When the door slammed shut behind me, she turned and said brightly, "Hello!" as though she expected a visitor. I took her hand and said "Bonjour, Madame Baker!" She invited me to sit while she sang another song.

We talked and laughed and she told me about her new show. It was to be a musical comedy of her long career from the time when she had left New York for Paris half a century before. I was impressed by her energy and readiness to talk about her life and promised to return for the opening of the new Revue called simply "Josephine." Nearly every notable French music-hall artiste had performed at the Bobino; Chevalier, Piaf, Montand, Regianni.... This hundred year old café-concert-hall was rooted in one of the older quarters of Paris and had always been frequented by amateurs of French song. Smaller than some of the central Paris theatres, the Bobino had gained a reputation for intimacy with its audience of more than a thousand spectators.

I returned to the Bobino theatre a week later to watch rehearsals for "Josephine" and sat discretely in the stalls. Josephine clearly galvanized everyone with her presence, gesturing and joking with the pianist, stage-hands, carpenters and casual visitors. Perhaps remembering I was waiting to hear more of her life and career, she suddenly shouted from the stage into the dark auditorium, "Where is that journalist?" I was afraid it was not the right time for an interview. I need not have worried. She called for my hand to help her step down from the stage and took me to a small office for a talk. The interview would be ready for the opening of "Josephine."

With word going round that there was a unique event taking place in Montparnasse, seats were sold out for "Josephine" weeks and months ahead, removing fears by the management that the public might not come to see an ageing music-hall star recall her past successes. The two producers at the Bobino, Dauzonne and Levasseur, believed they had a hit destined for a successful run. Plans were made to take the review to London and New York. Few of Josephine's immediate circle dared to express doubts that an artiste who was nearly 69 could sustain a new arduous tour abroad.

Josephine's Last Show

The gala opening of "Josephine" took place in an atmosphere of intense excitement. Fashionable "Le Tout Paris", including prominent personalities in French public life, converged on the small Paris theatre. My companion and I were seated near the veteran actor Michel Simon and other invited guests. A congratulatory telegram from President Valery Giscard d'Estaing was read out from the stage. It acknowledged Josephine's "universal talent" and spoke of a "grateful France whose heart has so often beaten with yours…," a reference to Josephine's services to France during the Second World War.

"Josephine" settled down to a" long, successful run," as they say in the profession. She danced, sang, clowned and was serious and sentimental, with as much energy and inspiration as she did, thirty, forty years ago when she was the star of the Casino de Paris and the

Folies Bèrgere. The audience gave her a standing ovation. Michel Simon was emotionally moved to leave his seat and climb on to the stage to embrace Josephine. The audience applauded the sight of two veteran performers together. It was to be the last appearances in public of two celebrated performers.

The end, when it came, was swift and not entirely unexpected. After a week of performances and a reception for three hundred guests at a Paris hotel, Josephine was believed to be sleeping when her telephone failed to respond to an interview with a journalist. She had suffered a heart attack. Doctors confirmed the cause of death as cerebral hemorrhage. Josephine's death was reported worldwide from the staid (and slightly inaccurate) Times of London to pages of photographs in the South American press. Critics and commentators recalled her self-appointed humanitarian mission for racial equality. Television and radio broadcasts recalled her musical career and life in France with her adopted family of orphans. My recent interview with her was an unexpected bonus for our programmes and the words and music of her song, "J'ai deux amours" was heard in all the media.

Chapter 7

"Words falling upon the facts like soft snow,
blurring their outlines and covering up all the details..."

George Orwell (1903-1950)

THE WEEKS AND MONTHS turned; a routine established itself: attendance at editorial meetings, union discussions and interviews outside the offices for the next programmed features. Natural disasters took their toll during 1975. Floods killed hundreds in India, a typhoon devastated 20,000 homes in Japan and at least 2,500 people died in an earthquake in eastern Turkey. While another General Assembly of the United Nations organisation was announced in New York, the city was once again declared financially bankrupt. Also in the United States the sporting event of the year was Muhammed Ali's victory over Joe Frazer for the world heavy-weight boxing title. And two women tried (unsuccessfully) to shoot President Gerald Ford.

Our presence in the studio for each live news broadcast was an acknowledgement there were people out there waiting for our words, as indeed the growing volume of listeners letters testified. D. Greenhall, a listener from Ancaster, Ontario, Canada wrote: "The programme I heard was very enjoyable and informative. A visit to the Eiffel Tower! You made it seem as though the listener was right there at the moment. It's programs like this which gives Short Wave Radio a good reputation."

With the premature death of Georges Pompidou and the election of Valery Giscard d'Estaing, French political life took on a new aspect.

Viewed as an "Atlanticist" in favour of the European Union, Giscard was an intellectual and an economist. From the moment he chose to walk up the Champs Elysées Avenue to the Arc de Triomphe with his ministers for his investiture, instead of using an open limousine, he had brought a new style of leadership to the role of French Head of State. The President's newly appointed government team of fifteen with Jacques Chirac as Prime Minister included only five Gaullists. The youngest French President in eighty years had brought new attitudes to a regime still viewed as Gaullist in spirit.

A shock for Parisians and tourists came on the French National Day celebrations when the traditional military parade with the white-hatted contingent of the French Foreign Legion, did not take place in the Champs Elysées Avenue but from Place de la Republique with no army tanks and fewer jet planes over-flying the parade on the 14th of July.

The President quickly brought reforms to the media. With the arrival of inexpensive battery-powered transistor receivers, radio was recognised as the ideal means of informing and motivating foreign populations with low levels of literacy. While the international war of the airwaves continued, the thirty year old ORTF (Office de Radio Television Française) was broken up into seven independent services. "Paris Calling Africa," begun in 1970, had become part of Paris Internationale in 1974 and RFI, Radio France Internationale was born and joined the throng of foreign language services of industrialised nations. But with fifteen languages, France was still far below the number of foreign languages broadcast daily by the U.S., Great Britain, the Soviet Union and China.

West European governments and France were striving for a measure of European unity, while minority groups were pulling in the opposite direction, trying to defend their separate identities. Basques and Bretons were clinging to their languages and folklore, while Corsicans fought to keep their independence of spirit within the French administration and the people of vanished Catalonia remembered when their language was spoken as far north as Limoges and Clermont-Ferrand. The President paid exceptional homage to Catalan culture when he invited musicians to play and sing at the Elysee Palace on French National Day.

Change of Neighbourhood

I was now living in the residential, sixteenth district of Paris north of the river, reputedly where the idle rich once lived in isolated splendour near the Boulogne Gardens. No longer! Once big apartments had been split into living-spaces called rentable "studettes," while their owners fled to the country. I rarely saw the nobleman-owner of my rented two-room flat who was usually absent in his country estate or abroad. His servants and I shared a wing of his apartment on the fifth-floor.

The view from the window of my new home was as theatrical as an old French movie by Marcel Carné. On one side there were zinc-grey rooftops and leaning chimneys stretching away to the western suburbs. On the other, beyond the local Town Hall clock-tower, I could just see the blunt top of the Arc de Triomphe at the head of the Champs Elysées Avenue. If I leant out dangerously on the balcony, I could also glimpse one splayed leg of the Eiffel Tower, illuminated at night like a giant brass souvenir. I could even see the top of the radio station among the high-rise buildings along the Seine. My small balcony became a third room in summer, with chairs and a table set among window boxes of geraniums, nasturtiums, lobelia and petunias. As a Briton abroad in a busy capital, I clung to the idea of keeping in touch with nature.

Physically, this district had not changed in half a century and has resisted developments that had transformed other former "villages" in the capital. Only the distant rumble of traffic on the ring-road across the Boulogne park remind me of other faces of Paris, of new tower blocks and crumbling tenements. The solid grey cliffs of the sixteenth district seemed to have escaped the planner's computer images of Manhattan-sur-Seine at La Défense. The entrance halls alone of nearby buildings are several times bigger than the one small room I had lived in across the river. The illusion of living in a traditional Haussmannian decor however was diminished by the sight of three giant satellite dishes stuck on a roof across the road from my window.

The crossroads near our house is the hub of the quarter. The Café de la Mairie stands on one corner; a butcher's shop occupies another. Two boulangeries facing each other on the other corners, close in rotation in summer to assure the supply of bread when small businesses pull down their shutters for the annual holidays. A little way down the street our local homeless 'clochard' squats outside the Spanish church looking submissive. Later, I saw him in the local bar refreshing himself for another stint of begging on the footpath. Further along the street, there were lines of cars with parking tickets fluttering from their windscreens. My Volkswagon was safely parked a kilometre away.

Recently, I had received a visit from a distinguished American art historian. Upon arrival, she strode speechless across the room and spreading her arms wide exclaimed, "Ah! This is Paris!" As the rags of evening clouds faded and a million lights replaced the grey roof-tops, I mentally echoed the song sung by that African-American singer, Josephine Baker. "J'ai deux amours, mon pays et Paris!" (Two loves have I, my country and Paris!)

In my new slightly larger living space and regular office hours, I needed help in keeping control of the accumulation of books and recordings from work. Offers of Home Help were frequent in this bourgeois district of well-furnished flats. I opted for an announcement in a local shop by a young woman named Dihya. After a telephone appointment, she began to visit me regularly to clean floors and kitchen-space for a modest monthly wage.

It was only later that I learned that Dihya was a talented singer who had needed occasional menial work to develop her musical career. A Berber of North African ethnic origin, Dihya had started to sing when young and had made her first record when a producer recognised the quality of her voice. Continuing to sing in the Berber language in France, she had become a symbol for Algerian youth in revolt searching for their cultural identity. Her record producer had left no time informing me that her first 45rpm single was quickly sold out. He explained that she preferred to sing in her native Berber, confident that she would leave her mark in North African culture. In Algiers, her singing voice was soon to be heard throughout North Africa and was to become a collector's item in France. We decided to add her voice in our programmes for other African listeners.

A Television First

Monday 16 July: I appeared live on National French colour television, to inaugurate the new series of evening news bulletins in English to keep summer visitors happy and informed. Handwritten text without a monitor but with a glance at the digital clock marking the time; it was a new challenge. It was a first in French TV history that inevitably provoked mild interest and curiosity. Comments about my necktie and the image of the Union Jack flag in the background, were among published remarks. The image of the British flag was interposed on the background and I was unaware of it. A chosen number of my colleagues followed me in rotation during the summer months.

The author inaugurates an English language broadcast of a French TV news programme.

The news content of our summer television programme was drawn from international events and French information. "France's new international airport is to open at Roissy, north-east of Paris. The traditional annual Tour de France cycle race was to pass through the United Kingdom and a stage in Plymouth had been included. And in Scotland the village blacksmith of Gretna Green has died prematurely at 45, after marrying 4,000 runaway couples in the last 12 years." It was an anecdote sure to amuse the non-French visitors to Paris. More than 16 million tourists were expected to visit France. The Secretary of State for Tourism revealed that the average tourist stayed only two and a half days in the capital.

Strolling down the avenues and boulevards early one morning after a night-shift, I was struck by the number of people already seated at leisure at café tables. There were also permanent groups standing or leaning at bars from early morning, confirming the image of French labourers having a drink on their way to work. Replying to a question in Parliament about alcoholism in France, said to cost the country more than fifty million dollars a year, Minister Michel Poniatowski suggested it might be desirable to ban the sale of alcohol in bars before ten in the morning. One could imagine the protests such a measure would arouse among bar owners and their customers.

As for the unhurried customers seated on café terraces, many were tourists or night-workers in service industries. In the notoriously difficult theatrical profession, out-of-work actors often claimed to be "just resting" while waiting for a role. Barmen had their own regular customers on their way to work whom they greeted daily. Waiters who served seated customers in boulevard cafés and restaurants were no longer addressed as "garcon" as was once the custom, but called a polite "Monsieur," as befitted their bow-ties and white aprons. The service charge for waiter-service is usually included in the bill, but an additional tip known as a "pour boire" (for a drink) was never refused and even politely demanded on occasion! I was even once chased across the boulevard in Clichy after omitting to leave a gesture of appreciation in a bar-restaurant.

My morning stroll brought me to the elegant Café de la Paix, on the corner of Place de L'Opera. As long ago as the reign of Louis-Phillipe (1773-1850) horse-drawn cabs used to drop passengers at a fashionable rendezvous called La Grange aux Belles which later became the celebrated Café de la Paix. Charles Garnier's new Opera House was then beginning to emerge. Garnier had won the competition for the new Paris Opera House initiated by Napoleon the Third. Napoleon's Spanish wife, the Empress Eugenie-Marie, interested herself in the project and was said to have asked Garnier in what style his design was to be.... Was it Louis 14, 15 or 16th style? Diplomatically, Garnier replied "It's in Napoleon the Third's style, Madame!"

Artists and their admirers had begun to frequent the café. Baron Haussemann's new avenues and boulevards brought more visitors to the district. The Café de la Paix began to reflect «la vie Parisienne» of the Belle Epoch. Edward VII, as Prince of Wales, dined there. Caruso sketched on the napkins and André Gide sat watching the passing crowds. Oscar Wilde, sitting on the terrace one day, thought he saw an angel on the wet roadway outside. It was but the reflection of the statuary on the summit of the facade of the Opera House! Today, the Café de la Paix stands at a busy intersection in the heart of the capital, with a tumult of traffic passing its doors. The distinguished visitors book records the names of Maria Callas, Arthur Rubenstein, Richard Nixon.... Prior to its restoration, the only time it was closed was the day World War II was declared. Later, General de Gaulle and his officers dined there in 1944 after the liberation of Paris.

My walk led me to the nearby Place Vendôme, a square surrounded by luxury shops and offices dominated by the historic Vendôme column dedicated to Napoleon's brilliant victory over Austria and Russia in 1805. Twelve hundred Russian and Austrian canons were melted to provide bronze for the sculpted shaft of the column. An elegant shop-front named Gélot Hatter displaying the British Royal Coat of Arms caught my eye. As I pushed open a heavy street door, a dark-suited businessman greeted me with "Bonjour, Monsieur!" In answer to my question, he explained that when King Edward VII of England was the Prince of Wales, he was received by the French President in 1905. Respectful of protocol, he had sought a suitable hat for the occasion. It was Monsieur Gélot who supplied one, thus legally earning him the title, "By Royal Appointment, Hatter to the King." American President Lyndon Johnson, the actor Sir Laurence Oliver and architect Frank Lloyd Wright were among later customers at Gélot's. As I left the Royal Hatter, I was told by the manager that many of the black berets worn in France were probably made in Great Britain! Could he have been referring to the London suburb of Wandsworth, I wondered, which was once famous for its hats in the early 18th century. He omitted to mention that the celebrated Polish musician Frederic Chopin had died in the same building more than 100 years earlier.

French "Hatter to King Edward VII" in central Paris.

Back at the news desk, I learned that Pablo Picasso had died at the age of ninety-two in the south of France. One of the best known artists of the century, he had spent most of his working life outside of his Spanish homeland. President Pompidou had officially opened a temporary exhibition of Picasso's work at the Louvre Museum to celebrate the artist's ninetieth birthday. His most famous work, Guernica was hanging in the Modern Art Museum in New York. Regarding cubism, Picasso's well-known picture called Demoiselles d'Avignon did not refer to the French town of that name but to a brothel in a street in Barcelona, Spain. The French State accepted death duties from Picasso's estate in the form of works of art and a donation of his work from his second wife Jacqueline. A museum in Paris devoted to his work was planned.

Picasso had always been a rich source of anecdote. Rumour and controversy had continuously surrounded him. The French poet, Jean Cocteau, called him a "sentimental mandolist and a fierce picador," but he was really neither. Picasso had never been a sentimentalist, in the sense that he never looked back. When the style or period of his work was finished, he always discarded it for something new. Cocteau's use of the word mandolist was a reference to the artist's use of that instrument as a motif in his early cubist paintings.... As to being a "fierce picador," Picasso was a strong partisan of what he believed in politically and artistically, but he could also be gentle and quixotic. A story was told about the owner of one of his paintings coming to him to have it authenticated because there had always been imitations of his work on the art market. When the owner of the picture asked Picasso to verify it as his work, Picasso refused, declaring it to be a fake! When the astonished owner protested that Picasso had indeed painted the picture, Picasso replied, "I often paint fakes!"

On a work-free Sunday, I decided to visit the former home of another celebrated painter who had made France his home, Vincent Van Gogh. He had later lived in a small town of Auvers-sur-Oise, north of Paris and was buried next to his brother Théo, in a nearby cemetery. Accompanied by Simon, our mime-actor colleague, we took the road north and visited the small hotel where Van Gogh had lived in his small room in the auberge with its single bed and chair he had painted. Later, we stood beside the twin graves of Vincent and Théo set against a wall beside other tombs. The parched landscape and dusty plain under twisting clouds we had driven through were as Van Gogh must have seen in his last days. As we drove home to Paris, I gathered a few stalks of wheat from the open hillside to catch a little of the atmosphere of that countryside.

Two worlds, the past and the present - I can move effortlessly between the two, on borrowed time. A book about Eton and I am dreaming among the willows on the banks of the river Thames in England. I think of my grandfather and see him sitting there painting among long grass and buttercups beside the slow-flowing river below that improbable Windsor castle perched on the hill. The thud of an oar from a skiff brings him back to his watercolours; the colour is drying and there's a fly caught in a pool of Prussian blue. He begins to mix the colours again, smooth the sky a little with delicate flowing strokes. And finally, he does what no purist would ever do, he adds a single white swan with a brush of pure flake white, drifting silently among the shadows and branches dipping beside the opposite banks of the river. Then he gathers up his things and walks slowly home to tea. I recall hearing the traditional song sung by students at Eton College.

The river Thames painting at Eton
painted by the author's grandfather.

Jolly boating weather, and a hay harvest breeze
Blade on the feather, shade off the trees;
Swing, swing together, with your bodies between your knees.
Others will fill our places, dressed in the old light blue;
We'll recollect our races, we'll to the flag be true
Youth will be in our faces when we cheer for an Eton crew.

--The Eton Boating Song

Today, the thunder rang and rain fell in the open courtyard of the Louvre Museum. Simon had accompanied me to interview two dancers of the Opera Ballet who were rehearsing for open-air performances of Swan Lake. Thirteen performances were planned on an open-air stage in the courtyard of the Louvre with Nureyev booked to dance every night with three different partners. Despite a free first-night on Bastille Day, the weather was cold and windy. Noella Pontoise and Patrice Bart were not visible in rehearsal. Suddenly, a figure I recognised strode sadly across the stage dragging a long coat behind him. Rudolf Nureyev stopped when I greeted him then abruptly strode on, clearly not wishing to talk. Simon and I left and later learned that the rehearsals and evening performance had been cancelled because of bad weather.

I recalled my first real meeting with Rudolf Nureyev in the 60's in Lebanon when he was starring with Margot Fonteyn in the ballet Giselle in an International Festival in Baalbek. We had met after the performance standing among the fallen columns of the historic, ancient Phoenician city. We chatted about the uniqueness of the huge Temple of Jupiter in which they had danced. Nureyev spoke in hesitant English while Fonteyn spoke with natural elegance. I remember the surprising fragility of her hand and wrists as we shook hands. Margot Fonteyn had been dancing Swan Lake since 1938, the year Rudolf was born. Despite the difference in their age, they were a celebrated couple from the London Royal Festival Ballet, after teaming up in Spoleto, Italy, following Nureyev's dramatic defection from the Russian Kirov Ballet in 1961.

Born a Muslim Tartar in Siberia in 1938, Nureyev had made a dramatic break from his country during a tour in France with the Russian Kirov Ballet in 1961, when he learned the Russians wanted his return home. KGB agents had tried to get him on a plane for Moscow from the Paris Le Bourget airport. French officials intervened and Nureyev was granted political asylum through the intervention of the British embassy in Paris. At the invitation of Ninette de Valois, the director of the London Royal Ballet, Nureyev partnered Margot Fonteyn in the ballet Giselle. Fonteyn was at first reticent of her partner who was almost twenty years her junior but their natural talent and love of the dance united them on the stage. They became a celebrated couple of the Festival Ballet touring the world. Nureyev later became

Director of the Paris Opera Ballet. He was not the only celebrity to leave the Soviet Union. Another leading dancer, Mikhail Baryshnikov defected from the Bolshoi Ballet while on tour in Toronto, Canada in June 1974.

A U.N. Mission

A sudden pause in world news at RFI and I am assigned to attend the 30th General Assembly of the United Nations in New York. The ceremony in mid-September promised to be a notable event with a growing number of Third World member countries calling for the redistribution of the world's wealth and resources.

After briefing and visa formalities, I am on the plane for New York. Time stands still as we prolong the European day by chasing the sun across the Atlantic. A taxi from Kennedy airport and I check in at the Pickwick Arms Hotel on East 51st Street. The giant tower of the UN building looms nearby on New York's East River. The thirty-nine floor building, housing multi-national delegates, receives more than a million visitors a year. I dutifully present my journalistic credentials to Mr. Richard Katangolé, the head guide of the Secretariat and was issued with authority to attend the 30th General Assembly of the World Body. I climb to the vast Delegates Lounge overlooking the river, decorated with a tapestry depicting the Great Wall of China. Groups of well-dressed delegates are preparing for the official opening that afternoon.

The hall of the General Assembly of the United Nations organisation recalls a classic Greek theatre in which performers and spectators are joined in architectural unity. Semi-circles of seats descend to a central rostrum and podium where the presiding President and his supporters face the assembly of more than a hundred delegates, each with a desk labelled with their country of origin. The inaugural session of the 30th General Assembly resembles a fashionable "first night" with men and women of every nationality shaking hands and greeting each other. The press and public gallery is packed with late-comers standing as the out-going President, Abdelaziz Bouteflicka takes his place on the central podium to open the inaugural session at 3:40 pm.

The routine business of the day is not without incident. Like a school roll-call a member of each of the 138 delegations present is called one-by-one to vote in the secret ballot to elect the new presiding President.

Each places their unidentified voting paper in a round box supported on thin legs like a conjurors equipment designed to demonstrate secrecy. When South Africa is called, a wave of muttering sweeps the assembly. An earlier Security Council meeting had condemned South Africa's policy of apartheid, or racial segregation. South Africa's continued disregard of the UN resolution had led to its suspension from last year's General Assembly. South African liberation movements in the special political committees of the UN had called for a boycott of sports events violating the Olympic Games principle of non-discrimination.

New York

"If there was ever an aviary over-stocked with jays it is that Yaptown-on-the-Hudson, called New York," wrote O. Henry in The Gentle Grafter. After long hours spent in the United Nations, I decided to explore the city. The streets of midtown Manhattan are thronged with business people pouring out of offices for a one-hour lunch break. American businessmen appear to work harder and with more determination than their French counterparts. To avoid traffic congestion, many work late in the evening to accomplish more.

Food can be a problem if one comes from the land of haute cuisine. Many restaurants offer foreign menus and prices vary from reasonable to monstrous. "Little France, Little Italy, Chinatown, Africa," they are all here. I visit a Lexington Avenue coffee shop, then take a high-chair at a Schraffts counter. Two blocks off Broadway, I find "Chez Napoleon," a restaurant run not by a Corsican but a Breton family!

A tour of Harlem with Mr. Penelopé's Company to view black and Puerto Rican ghettos among African communities. The 7th Annual African-American Parade was due on Sunday September 14th. I attended a first-night in a Broadway theatre of "Ah, Wilderness" by Eugene O'Neil. Total informality of dress and manners, jeans and open-neck shirts, talk! One man never removes his cowboy hat! Then the weekend press, scores of English, Chinese, Hebrew and Italian editions each weighing kilos!

A guitarist sings in an open forecourt, People Talk About New York!

People talk about New York,
Detroit's alright, Pennsylvania's a mania,
Then there's Kentucky, which is lucky
And Charlestown is a wild town,
They say Oregon's moribund
But for a walk, it's New York
Until Wall Street begins to pall
For me it's New York. I'm caught!

I could not leave New York before viewing the Statue of Liberty, standing at the entrance of the harbour. Liberty Enlightening the World, by the French sculptor Frédéric Auguste Bartholdi, was a gift from France to celebrate the centenary of American Independence. Its inauguration took place on October 28, 1886, with the French tricolour flag covering the crowned head of the world's biggest statue of a woman that had greeted thousands of sea-borne immigrants to the U.S. for more than a century. I took the ferry to Bedloe's Island and joined other visitors to the monument. Of the thousands who seek a closer look at Liberty Enlightening the World, I learned that very few New Yorkers ever pay a visit to the statue whose image is known worldwide.

The colossal scale of the statue only becomes evident when one begins to climb inside from the base up to the body and head of the woman holding the Torch of Freedom more than three hundred feet above the harbour. From a circular stairway within her head, one views New York Bay from circular windows within her crown. Bartholdi had given Lady Liberty a right arm forty-three feet long holding the torch of freedom while her left hand clasps the Declaration of Independence with a forefingers eight feet long. Other measures are equally surprising: Liberty's nose is four feet from top to chin, while each of Liberty's fingernails are larger than the sleeve of a long playing record. The final full scale statue for New York was not achieved without problems. Originally financed by a Franco-American committee, work was interrupted by lack of private funds, Gustave Eiffel took over the project which was finally dismantled and shipped to New York in 214 cases for a dedication ceremony in 1886.

Back in Paris, I take a closer look at a smaller copy of the New York statue standing at the end of Swans Island on the River Seine opposite the French Radio Station. The 11.5 meter model facing west on the river was dedicated in 1889. It was one of several preliminary models Bartholdi made in his workshop in western Paris in collaboration with the French engineer Gustave Eiffel. Another smaller replica of the New York statue stands in the Luxembourg Gardens in the Paris Latin Quarter. It is among several models Bartholdi originally conceived for the entrance of the Suez Canal to proclaim "Liberty Towards Asia." Bertholdi finally settled for New York in the United States.

Frédéric Bartholdi's model of Liberty standing on an island on the Seine.

Bartholdi left a strong legacy of art and history in French provincial centres. In the southwestern city of Bordeaux, a replica of Liberty was destroyed by the Nazis during World War II, to be replaced with a plaque commemorating the victims of the September 11th, 2001 terrorist attacks in New York. Yet another copy of Liberty appeared in the centre of the southern French town of Saint-Cyr-sur-Mer near Marseilles. There is a 12 meter replica of the Statue of Liberty in Colmar,

Bartholdi's birthplace, dedicated on July 4th, 2004, to commemorate the one hundredth anniversary of the sculptor's death.

Bartholdi's bronze copy of his Lion of Belfort, dedicated to Colonel Denfert-Rochereau, who defended the city of Belfort against the Prussians in 1870-1871, stands to this day at a busy road junction in southern Paris near the entrance to the Catacombs in the 14th district of the capital. Bartholdi's Lion of Belfort stands carved out of living rock in the eastern French city of Belfort. The Bartholdi Museum in Colmar contains early working models he made during the designing of his masterpiece.

Chapter 8

"The subway system does away with speech; you don't have to speak either when you pay or when you get in or out. Because it is so easy to understand, the subway is a frail and hopeful stranger's best chance to think that he has quickly and correctly, at the first attempt, penetrated the essence of Paris."

Franz Kafka

PRESIDENT POMPIDOU LEFT A large legacy of urban developments in Paris and suburbs. Historically bounded by ancient walls and barriers, the capital was struggling to accommodate a growing population and work-force drawn to the "Ile de France" region. New suburban business centres had emerged to be served by Métro lines. In Paris, an operation of "Haussemannian" proportion was taking place thirty meters below the former central food market "Les Halles." A Métro exchange centre, reputed to be the world's biggest underground rail station, was planned to carry more than 800,000 commuters daily to and from the capital. It was a key central part of the capital's Regional Express network. Meanwhile, the construction of a new Cultural and Arts Centre called the Pompidou Centre, near the Paris City Hall, had added to the growing turmoil in the city centre in the 1970's.

The former President's tolerance of the automobile was well known. When the new Paris ring-road was completed in April 1973, he had exclaimed publicly, "The French love their motorcars!" There were rumours that the Saint Martin canal, where loaded barges from the north wait at lock gates to join the Seine in Paris, might soon be drained and paved to become a new motorway. A fast motorway beside the northern banks of the Seine in Paris now offered motorists an unobstructed fourteen kilometre west-east crossing of the capital. Caricaturists quickly mocked the idea that cars might soon be streaming through the west-front doors of Notre-Dame cathedral!

One of the side issues resulting from the increase in vehicular traffic was the belief that cities were for cars and pedestrians were out of place and must be herded, or at best tolerated to give priority to motor vehicles. A partial ban on traffic in the historic Ile de Saint-Louis in the centre of Paris was introduced to preserve the character and atmosphere of that residential island. The move was endorsed by residential owners of property but opposed by local shops and restaurants. Such a conflict of interests did not arise in the newly emerging western business centre of La Défense where full acceptance of motor vehicles was incorporated in the ground plan of the quarter with its underground Métro service.

Paris was also going underground with underpasses and parking spaces and roads had started to dip into tunnels. Nearly ten thousand private and municipal parking spaces were slated to be built under the city's parks and avenues. Meanwhile, 30,000 new French francs bought a private parking space under the aristocratic Avenue Foch and a four-level public parking space below the historic Vendome Square could accommodate nine-hundred vehicles.

While the use of private motor vehicles Paris increased, so too did the incidents of accidents and injury, not to mention the health risks from air pollution. Policemen on point duty at the busy road intersection on the Champs Elysées Avenue had their tour of duty changed every three hours to avoid their near collapse from car exhaust fumes. Most serious accidents in Paris occurred on the newly completed ring-road encircling the capital where drivers drove faster without constraints of cross-roads and traffic lights. Road deaths in France, in which both commercial and private vehicles were involved, became head-line stories in national newspapers. A typical report announced thirty-eight road deaths in one week and illustrated "black spots" in Paris where nearly one hundred deaths a year were recorded.

Pedestrians were not forgotten in the growing risks from motor traffic on French roads. The Pedestrian Rights Association had called for a wide range of measures designed to protect non-motorised citizens. I was received by the newly elected President of the Association, Mr. Roger Lapeyre, in his office in the busy Latin Quarter. We talked about the aims and objectives of the association including speed limits near schools and stronger penalties for infringements. Mr. Lapeyre acknowledged the growing dominance of the automobile and manufacturers' seduction of the public at trade fairs and on television. At the close of our meeting I was invited to take a drink with Mr. Lapeyre in a bar near his office. As we waited patiently at a pedestrian crossing to cross the boulevard, we were nearly touched by an impatient private motorist.

Edith Piaf, France's Little Sparrow

The memories of many popular French personalities are ever present in Paris city life. I had arrived too late to see Piaf, Cocteau and Colette in action. Edith Piaf, one of France's most popular singers and Jean Cocteau, dramatist, poet and filmmaker, died within days of each other in 1963 and marked the end of an epoch in French life, art, letters and music. Both paid heavily with their health; Cocteau became seriously ill while making his celebrated film "La Belle et la Bête" (Beauty and the Beast), while Edith Piaf had so many breakdowns that audiences often wondered if she would finish a public performance on the stage. The singer who became a star after childhood near- blindness, accidents and illnesses, had captured the affection of thousands at home and abroad.

News of a Franco-American film of her life alerted me to the story of the girl who once sang for centimes in the cobbled streets of Belleville in Paris. "Piaf" was being filmed in its natural Paris setting. The story of La Môme is based on a biography written by Piaf's half-sister, Simone Berteaut. Together they had lived like vagabonds until Edith was acclaimed for her dramatic and emotional rendering of such songs as "Non, je ne regrette rien" and "La Vie en Rose." Before observing the film unit at work, I sought out her half-sister Simone and with Berteaut's book in my hand I visited her to hear more of their early life together. Huge photographs of Edith stared down at us from the walls of her home as Simone talked about their life half a century earlier. As we sat in the gloom of her modern first-floor flat, far from Belleville, I had the impression that Edith was alive and well.

Over in the eastern Paris quarter of Belleville, I found the film team working in a secluded courtyard of old buildings under the direction of Guy Casaril, who was trying to have television aerials removed from some roofs of homes for historic images of the epoch. Among a group of elderly neighbours present there were some who remembered Piaf and regarded her as their own. Simone Berteaut was there sitting on a stool watching the filming process and offering comment. A young actress was attempting to adopt attitudes of the singer as Piaf's recorded voice echoed eerily among the buildings. She knew the words of the songs but lacked the natural stridency and energy of the young Piaf. An associate American producer sat hopefully observing the filming process as a chapter of French entertainment history was recreated in a quarter already surrounded by modern high-rise buildings.

Piaf, Cocteau, Colette, all were gone before I arrived in France. Everywhere one went their presence was still felt in reference to their life and creative work. The singing voice of Piaf pervaded public places; Cocteau's words and images were ever present, and women's search for freedom and identity often led one back to Sidonie-Gabrielle Colette, the foremost French writer of her epoch.

I sought out Maurice Goudeket, Colette's last husband, on the occasion of the publication of his memoirs entitled, "Close to Colette." A bilingual journalist and writer himself, he received me in his flat near the Arc de Triomphe. Sixteen years her junior, Mr. Goudeket recounted their thirty years together until her peaceful death in 1954. His own life had been eventful having survived the war in France following his arrest and internment. Married to Colette in 1935, Maurice Goudeket recounted what he called "years of unclouded happiness" when he declared, "She enabled me to live in an enchanted world and offered me a picture of such greatness that I despair of being able to bear witness to it, although at least I have tried."

Maurice Goudeket then recalls, "I could not take my eyes off that most individual profile of hers, with the eyes set so expressively in the shadow of a lock of ash blond hair, the nose rather long at its end, the wide cheek bones, the thin bow of the mouth and the pointed chin. She shot me a look as blue as night, ironical and quizzical but with an indefinable nostalgia in it too. Something countrified and healthy emanated from her." As his cultured voice rolled on without hesitation,

I reflected on the chance that enabled me to share in a part of French literary history.

Maurice Goudeket and Colette experienced brief involvement in the war during the German occupation when they took part in international broadcasts from Paris. The Goudekets went on the air between midnight and four in the morning. Once a week, they drove through an eerie autumnal fog to the radio station. What Colette loved best about this brief patriotic service was to watch the dawn reflected in the waters of the Seine as they drove home.

Colette took her pen name from her father's surname who was a French government official in Burgundy. She left the region at eighteen to marry a Parisian writer and journalist named Willy. He persuaded her to writer stories which he corrected and sold under his own name! They separated and Colette entered the music-hall as a mime and nude dancer but continued to write, notably about animals, childhood memories and Parisian life, with analyses of emotion and sensual pleasure. Her novels such as "Cheri" and the "Claudine" series were established and "Gigi" later became a celebrated motion picture.

My nearest neighbour in my new quarter was now Krystyna, who was born in England of Polish parents, spoke French fluently and felt culturally European. She had joined us at the radio station for occasional translations and began to interview chosen personalities. She translated for the French Foreign Ministry and gave lessons in English for employees at the Bank of France. An expert in languages, she was soon to be featured in the daily L'Aurore newspaper with a photograph and headline, "It's Miss Onomatopées!" We lived in the fashionable west of Paris where many personalities had sought escape from the stress of the city centre.

Sunday morning in the Bois de Boulogne gardens, I strolled beside the lake and saw a couple I recognised. Jean Louis Barrault was taking the air arm-in-arm with Madeline Renauld. They both nodded graciously as I greeted them. Two emblematic figures from theatre and film taking their leisure among neighbours. I recalled my meeting with Barrault when he was rehearsing at the Orsay Theatre, in company with Krystyna when we had a pleasant conversation.

Pathé News in Montmartre

One of the interesting jobs that came my way in the 1970's was to translate and present the Pathé news feature in English for distribution abroad. The work involved being present in the Pathé recording studios in Montmartre from eight o'clock in the morning when the latest edition was run through for rehearsal and timing. The Pathé studios in Montmartre had a long history going back to the turn of the century when early classics of the Seventh Art were created by Robert Bresson, Marcel Carné and Jean Renoir. Among the last great names to have worked in the studios, Frederico Felleni had made "La Dolce Vita" and Luchino Visconte "Le Guépard." The building was later turned into the Femis Cinema School before becoming a commercial recording studio.

The text I hold in my hand is the result of several days work of translation. The two producers are waiting for me at their console. I enter the tiny recording booth and check the switch that puts my voice on the sound track. A voice test, a test run of some sequences, and I shorten a few lines to accommodate the sequence. The switch in my hand warns the recording technician that I am about to speak. The volume of background sounds is reduced. With half an eye on the projected image, I attempt to match the mood of the sequence scene by scene. The paragraphs of my text are numbered to coincide with the images and length of each sequence. The translations from the French are usually shorter and summarise the essence of the subject. There are occasional re-takes if my voice overlaps a change of image. Sometimes a halt is called for technical reasons.

One of my first reactions when presenting Pathé News in English was to attempt to imitate the tone of commentators I had long been familiar with in newsreels. Correct pronunciation of unfamiliar names and an appropriate tone of authority has to be respected. I hardly see the details of the images but guess the content. Most newsreels are similar; faces, action, long-shot, close-up and a shot and image to conclude. The scene changes, a page is turned, Comes The End! "OK, that's good. Thanks John." Another nights work is in the bag. I take off for a walk through Montmartre to home.

Africa Again

Every head of state makes official visits to other world capitals for prestige reasons or to attend international functions. As the pace of French life quickened, Africa loomed large again, not the desert wastes of central Africa but in the flourishing West African Republic of the Ivory Coast. I was briefly assigned to the French Presidential Association for a ten-day official visit to the Ivory Coast at the invitation of President Felix Houphouet-Boigny. It was VGE's first visit to one of the most developed countries on the Guinea coast.

A quick look at radio archives of France's former West African Empire and I learned that the country, independent from France since 1960, was rich in food and raw materials and supplied ingredients for more than half the world's chocolate. Abidjan the capital, a port linking a lagoon to the ocean, was once a port of slave-traders and owes its name to the pronunciation "m'bidjan" in the local Ebrié language. More than ten thousand French residents continued to use French currency.

At an official meeting at the Foreign Ministry, I am called aside by Monsieur Foccart, known as Mr. Africa, one of the founders of SAC, the "Action Civique," a secret force set up by General de Gaulle. As General Secretary of French-African relations, Mr. Foccart clearly wanted to meet the English journalist who addressed the African continent daily from French overseas radio. A brief walk together in the gardens of the ministry and Mr. Africa was assured of my loyalty to our mission. After an editorial briefing in the office and medical advice against catching yellow fever, we are issued with instructions concerning formal dress including dark suits and bow ties for official receptions.

I joined a team of international journalists on the plane for the Guinea coast known as the "white man's grave," where it is hotter in January than in August and prepare to join French overseas residents enduring the annual tropical dry-season. On arrival, the blanket heat of Abidjan confined us to air-conditioned buses and the hotel. From our 30th floor rooms, the capital appeared to be still emerging from pre-colonial days with high-rise office towers overshadowing former residential districts.

Our time was quickly filled with official receptions. The motorcade to and from our hotel became a ritual procession watched by thousands of black smiling faces with drumming and chanting in the streets.

After a reception at the French Embassy, we visit Yamoussoukro, the birthplace of Felix Houphouet-Boigny, north of the capital. On the road out of the capital, wide well-surfaced streets with footpaths and traffic lights at each junction of roads leading to the interior countryside but all were deserted with no motor vehicles or pedestrians in sight. A strange city with apparently no sign of becoming a busy capital.

Our host President remained a popular leader since the country's independence from France. Houphouet-Boigny became the first African member of the French cabinet and the former colony's representative in the French National Assembly. He maintained a palace at his birthplace surrounded by a crocodile-infested moat. Reception at the palace was followed by a lake-side garden party. I treasured the gift of a small ivory statuette handed to me by the President at the close of the reception.

Before returning to France, I regretted not having seen a celebrated Liana Bridge, a locally created way of crossing rivers from opposite banks. These suspended swaying walkways are fashioned secretly at night by villagers who jealously conceal the traditional skills they use to create Liana bridges which are considered sacred by the population. In my brief visit to this other world, I never saw an elephant for an instant or witnessed the Feast of the Yams, held annually in February, or even a performance of the internationally known Sénoufo Dancers or Senia as this northern ethnic race call themselves. Another time perhaps!

Back in the "City of Light," I reflected on the diversity of origins of Parisians in our crowded capital and what Paris had been like in the Twenties when Josephine Baker had made her sensational appearance in 1925. Many other American and European performers and musicians had discovered France between the two world wars and vestiges of that period were still visible in French culture in the arts, music and literature. While West European governments are striving for European unity, minority groups in France seem to be tugging the other way. Basques and Bretons cling to their language and folklore while Corsicans keep their independence of spirit and the people of vanished Catalonia remember when their language was spoken as far north as Limoges and Clermont-Ferrand.

Visitors to Paris often stop in front of Shakespeare and Company in the Latin Quarter out of curiosity or to observe the decorative façade of the bookshop facing Notre Dame cathedral. Many had read about the shop in guidebooks or had heard about it by word of mouth. The establishment had become a favoured meeting place and centre of literary creativity for more than half a century. Originally a simple English language bookshop, it had enlarged and developed into a cultural meeting place of writers of all categories beginning with poets. Many celebrated writers began their careers under the Shakespeare sign and often returned to thank George Whitman, the owner who had offered them hospitality in his five-floor building which included a library for consultation and study and a small room full of children's books.

The first time I met George Whitman, he was sitting behind the cash desk of his bookshop near the river Seine, observing customers who came and went, not always buying a book but exploring the Latin Quarter. Its free and easy atmosphere was unlike other shops only interested to sell their products and services to make a profit. The district was dense with restaurants, bars, souvenir shops and hotels along the Left Bank.

The Seine and the cathedral and churches were backdrops to a busy tourist quarter where scores of "bouquinists" lined the banks of the river selling second-hand books, postcards and souvenirs from improvised wooden sheds along the river front. That was perhaps why George Whitman bought his small bookshop at the base of a five-floor building once a part of a monasterial complex next to the historic church of Saint Julien-le-Pauvre.

One day in the Latin Quarter, I visited the shop whose boxes of books were strewn on the footpath, competing with traditional second-hand book dealers along the riverside. I found George Whitman seated behind his cash-desk, ready to help customers looking for books of fiction, history, biography, poetry.... I was sure to find vestiges of that past of Paris among the crowded shelves of all categories of literature including Spanish, German and Russian volumes. Mr. Whitman took me to his small annex of the shop called "Antiquarian Books" and I learned something about the history of the establishment.

George Whitman is often visible in front of his bookshop.

Born in Salem, Massachusetts, USA, George Whitman was a compulsive traveller who came to France in 1946. He attended the Sorbonne University where he gained a diploma of "Civilisation" studies. He began a small lending library of American GI's who had stayed in France after the war. He then bought a small Arab grocery shop on the front of the Seine in 1951. Originally called The Mistral, after the dry winds that blow across southern France, he began to acquire books and develop the floors above the shop. He changed the name to Shakespeare and Company, derived from the original shop of that name created in 1919 by another American, Sylvia Beach, in a street near the Odeon

Theatre. Sylvia Beach was the first to publish James Joyce's "Ulysses" in an issue of one thousand copies on the 2nd of February, 1922. A close friend of Sylvia Beach, Adrienne Monnier was to publish a sample of "Ulysees" in her French magazine "Commerce" in 1924.

Chapter 9

"The most difficult character in comedy is that of the fool, and he must be no simpleton that plays that part."

Miguel de Cervantès, Spanish author, dramatist (1547-1616)

WALKING DOWN A TREE-LINED avenue with Simon after a dayshift at the radio station, my colleague suddenly stopped and gave a spontaneous demonstration of what he was learning at the Paris International Mime School. Arms, legs and facial grimaces suddenly halted passers-by who stared, convinced that it was a private joke. I knew of Simon's studies under Marcel Marceau but had never seen the master clown on the stage. He was known around the world but little talked about. Clearly the art of mime has its mysteries. A visit to the International Mimeograph Company on an open public day near Republic Square in Paris offered me a glimpse of the creative energy harnessed by the greatest mime artist in the western world. I asked to have a private interview with Monsieur Marceau and was invited to his office.

Marcel Marceau

The Paris Mime School was where Marcel Marceau taught and performed when he was not on tour as Mr. Bip, the character he created in his performances. The father of four children liked talking not only in his native French but also in English in which he was fluent. Unfazed by the microphone in my hand, he recalled his career as the world's most famous clown. Born in Strasbourg, eastern France, he decided to become an actor when he was twenty and attended Charles Dullin's Drama School, before becoming a mime student under Etienne Decroux. He then set up his own mime school in Paris in 1978.

Having already watched him performing silently on the stage with his students before interviewing him, I asked the first innocent question that came into my head: "Is there anything that you cannot express in mime?" Without hesitation he replied "Yes, lies!" (laughing) "Because you have to speak to be a liar. What words best express are LIES!"

Marcel continued: "I don't think about words when I write a story. The story gives the idea to translate into gestures what writers do with words. It's not important what the characters say, it's how they behave. The problem with mime is to choose subjects which are better expressed in silence, because mime is beyond words. A mime is also an actor but he is a physical actor. From 1947 until today, I never spoke on the stage except twice…. Once I played in *L'Historie de Soldat* by Stravinski and *Ramuz* (1955). I was the Devil and it was a speaking role and I was miming and speaking. The other one was when I said, "No!" in Mel Brooks' film called, *The Silent Movie*. It's beautiful to be able to communicate without words and through my silent adventures I can perform in 80 countries, ten times in the five continents…. I knew that one doesn't laugh in English or French or Japanese or Chinese or Russian. And that is why I think that mime, like music, transcends the human soul and feelings and it has become a universal art."

Throughout the three quarters of an hour that we were together, his earnest conversation flowed without stopping and it was remarkable for the lack of gestures with his hands, so typical of the French manner of communication. His gaze was direct and unflinching. His English was almost perfect. His appreciation of the philosophy of theatre and mime was deep and incredibly impressive.

The atmosphere of dedicated hard work in the mime school was exemplified by a lone student in rehearsal, twisting in silent absorption over an idea to be expressed in movement and another student I nearly fell over, who was sleeping under a blanket among the banks of empty seats. Outside, the sun shone and people moved about in the streets, walking, stooping, bumping into each other and gesticulating in that artless way we all have when we are at a loss for words or simply tired.

Not so Marceau. He displayed none of the complex attitudes so evident in many theatrical people who seek to ingratiate themselves. Marceau seemed only interested in conveying an idea as precisely as possible without impatience about questions that have been put to him for half a century. He talked about Marcel Marceau as though detached from the man who bore his name and who, in turn had invented Mr. Bip. I wondered what another celebrated French creator would have made of Marceau's career.

One might be temped to think that such revered personalities as Charles Chaplin and Maurice Chevalier no longer have anything to offer us because they are no longer before the public after a long life of activity. One of Chaplin's early full-length films called Modern Times has recently been reissued in France. The film made in 1933 had not been seen for half a century. On the eve of the reopening of Modern Times in the Champs Elysées Avenue, Charles Chaplin was reported to have said, "France has a special meaning for me. I think the French understand my films better than anyone else." The character personified in his films recalls optimism and humour in the face of adversity in troubled times. Chaplin personally attended the revival in France of ten of his early films and was greeted by Ministers and the City Fathers, many of whom had grown up with the voices of Piaf, Trenet and Chevalier.

Alexander Dumas

There's a familiar saying in French: "Chacun son métier," meaning, roughly, "Each to his own job," or "You do your job and leave me to do mine!" France's celebrated author, Alexander Dumas, discovered this one day during rehearsals of his play The Three Musketeers. Dumas became puzzled when a backstage fireman would always disappear during every rehearsal at the beginning of the seventh act. From curiosity, Dumas went in search of the man and found him in a nearby bistrot.

"Why do you always leave your post in the theatre at the same moment everyday during rehearsals?" The man replied that part of the new play was so boring he always chose to leave for a glass of red wine. Dumas rushed back to the theatre, grabbed a script and promptly changed the seventh act. When the astonished company asked what was wrong, Dumas replied, "If it doesn't amuse the fireman, then it won't amuse the audience!" And he then proceeded to rewrite the whole act. Alexander Dumas knew how to take advice from an amateur critic but probably could not have put out a fire by himself.

Pompidou Centre

Paris has long been noted for its fine buildings and historic monuments but the names of individual creators are less well known than the French leaders who gave their names to projects which outlived them. French political leaders often leave their names on an edifice to mark their term of office. Avenues and squares are often named in homage to their role and services to the State but the architect they commission often remains unknown to the public. This was not the fate of the Anglo-Italian architects who designed and built the Pompidou Centre in Paris, initiated by a president who died before seeing the realization of his dream. The architects of that controversial building, Richard Rogers and Renzo Piano, later continued to work and enjoy their notoriety in France and many other countries.

The Georges Pompidou Centre in central Paris.

The history of the Pompidou Centre dates from 1937 when the Paris municipal authorities acquired a Square known as the "Plateau Beaubourg," named after the village "Le Beau Bourg," which had existed since the 11th century. Local homes, no longer habitable, had since been abandoned and demolished and the resulting space, the size of several football fields, had become a parking area near the Paris City Hall. The site now sandwiched between the historic Marais quarter and the emerging Forum of Les Halles next to the church of Saint Eustache, appeared an ideal location for the erection of a cultural arts centre.

A development project had been discussed by De Gaulle's Cultural Minister, Andre Malraux and the innovative Swiss-born architect, Charles-Edouard Jeanneret (Le Corbusier) had even been consulted. The development project had already provoked comment for or against a multi-story building to house an Arts and Cultural Centre. An early competition document had suggested that "the Plateau Beaubourg be developed as a live Centre of Information covering Paris and beyond."

President Pompidou's declared determination to create a cultural centre in which the plastic arts are joined to music, the cinema, books and audio research, generated more than six hundred design projects from forty-nine countries. When the accepted project was chosen, Richard Rogers and Renzo Piano jointly began work in 1972. Not since the Eiffel Tower was built in 1879 has a new structure in Paris provoked such interest. It was the first major project devoted to the living arts in France since the beginning of the century. Also included in the project was an underground Musical Research Institute and Acoustic Research Centre known by the initials IRCAM.

The published conception of the new Arts Centre quickly provoked comment and criticism. Its severely functional appearance presented a large building with no conventional façade or entrance. The huge steel and glass skeleton rose among centuries-old grey streets and buildings. All access stairways and services were visible on the outside of the structure. In answer to critical comparisons to "an oil refinery," Richard Rogers replied that "buildings can harmonise by contrast and not only by inspiration of a style." With so many structural elements of steel and glass crossing the exterior, critics were quick to suggest that the new Pompidou Centre could become as big a maintenance problem as the Eiffel Tower in order to protect it from rust and ruin.

Several thousand people converged on the central arrondissement of the capital for the official opening of the new centre while several hundred invited guests waited inside the main hall for the inauguration ceremony chaired by President Giscard d'Estaing. Entering privately from the street level in Rue Saint Denis, I joined other invited journalists while ministers and officials took their place on a platform.

As we stood beneath a huge photo image of the man who had given his name to the centre, I found myself next to someone I recognized standing anonymously in the crowd. "Good evening, Mr. Heath!" I said politely to the former British Prime Minister. He turned to me smiling and in answer to my question, Mr. Edward Heath replied that it was normal that he should honour the event for the Frenchman he had known and admired.

Art lover, musician and orchestral conductor, Edward Heath was not the only musician to become a political leader of his country. I recalled that Ignace Pederewski, pianist, composer and statesman, also became Prime Minister of Poland in 1919. It was Edward Heath who insisted on bringing his own Steinway piano to No. 10 Downing Street when he came to office in London. As he had once said, "Music can work miracles on each of us if we give it a chance. Music can triumph over the conflicts of mankind."

Speeches for the opening ceremony paid homage to Georges Pompidou's own respect of the creative arts. As I left the crowded assembly, I recalled that both Pompidou and Heath had expressed agreement over Britain's full membership in the emerging European Community. Addressing the Parliament in London, P.M. Heath had asserted that the Concorde aircraft and the Channel Tunnel were both necessary for the economic health of Great Britain and France.

A Mayor of Paris

Following the establishment of the Pompidou Centre, Paris endured a second innovation in 1977 when, on the initiative of President Giscard d'Estaing, Paris adopted its first-ever mayor of the capital. For more than a century, the city had been administered by a government-appointed Préfet. The power and influence of the former Préfet had often been beneficial to the city. It was Baron Haussmann, under Napoleon III who had reshaped the capital in 1870, giving Paris wide, straight boulevards, noble vistas and monuments. It was said in good humour that the only thing Haussmann did not straighten was the course of the River Seine! If some of his sweeping changes had been achieved un-democratically, the long-term results were largely appreciated.

Following a heated electoral campaign, former Prime Minister Jacques Chirac was elected the first Mayor of Paris since the Revolution. The President viewed the historic appointment as a move towards decentralization on a level with other major French cities. With authority over a hundred thousand municipal employees and three million inhabitants of the city, the power and prestige of the new Mayor of Paris was also a potential challenge to the role of the President. As the main pole of attraction for social, economic and artistic activities and the seat of government, the creation of a mayor for the capital was a move to reaffirm the position of Paris among world great cities. A page had been turned in the history of the French capital.

The City of Light

Listeners to our programmes, including those to my regular contribution to Australian radio, often asked why Paris was called "The City of Light." Many capital cities have historic labels such as "Rome the Eternal City" or "Jerusalem, City of Peace." Paris, City of Light has nothing to do with the quality of the air on a spring morning or the historic buildings and monuments that were scrubbed clean on the orders of Minister Malraux. The term "Paris, City of Light" owes its origin to a simple historic fact: it was the first great city in the world to have street lighting. It was during the last period of the reign of Louis XIV that some 6,000 lanterns were placed along the wider avenues of the capital to make Paris safer for citizens who walked at night. The innovation brought provincials and foreigners to stare at the city which appeared ablaze with light at dusk. But there were other more recent claims to the title "City of Light."

The principle of gas lighting was invented by the French engineer, Philip Lebon, and in 1817 his "thermo-lampe" was installed in a coffee-shop named "Café du Gaz Eedrogene." Ironically, Philip Lebon was stabbed to death one night in the Champs Elysées Avenue before gas street lighting appeared all over the city. A century later, another Frenchman made his contribution to the City of Light with the first-ever neon electric sign over a barber shop. It displayed the words "Palace Coif-er" in 1912. It was Jacques Fonseque who developed the gas "neon" for lighting which first appeared at No.14 in the Boulevard Montmartre. Paris, City of Light continues to impress visitors even in the shadow of search lights from the top of the Eiffel Tower and the annual Christmas decorations in the Champs Elysées Avenue.

Istanbul

Foreign listeners to our programs are delighted to meet in person the voices they recognize on the air when they visit Paris. The pleasure was mutual and offered us valuable information about their country and how our programs were received. It was rare for us to visit one of our regular correspondents. I decided to take a break from routine and together with Krystyna, we took a plane to Turkey to visit Mr. Jacques Fis in the Yesilkoy suburb of Istanbul. From our hotel in Istanbul, we took a taxi to the suburban home of Jacques Fis and were greeted at his door. He had been expecting us and we already had a lot in common from his letters. We quickly accepted the fact that our fluent Turkish listener was almost sightless. Jacques showed us his equipment that enabled him to listen to foreign radio programs and we spent a pleasant afternoon with our Turkish listener before returning to Istanbul to view at a distance the new bridge spanning the Bosphoros that was to join Europe and Asia.

Not surprisingly, Radio Australia wanted to know something about French fashion houses that frequently informed the press about their latest creations in photographs and forecasts. Reard, the French fashion house that had launched the "bikini" in 1946 was reported to be threatened with closure. The world's smallest bathing costume, a woman's two-piece bathing suit that left most of the wearer uncovered, came from the Marshall Islands

The author on a visit to Istanbul.

and was named after the Pacific atoll before the U.S. carried out its first nuclear tests.

Although French fashion houses work all the year round to present their collections to the trade and media, the women who do the sewing are called "midinettes" because they only stopped work at noon for a one-hour break from their labours. The heritage of French fashion began in the Court of Versailles where Napoleon, like King Louis XIV, realized that fashion was a way to establish privilege. Everyone at Court tried to copy what the King wore and he scolded the wives of his Generals if they wore the same dress twice. With the French Revolution, the centre of French fashion moved to Paris and became "Haute Couture" popular under the second Empire. The Empress Eugenie, wife of Napoleon III, helped boost the textile industry in the city of Lyon. Today's blue denims owe its origin to the town of Nimes, from the French term "de nimes!

Of the hundreds of letters addressed to Radio France International's foreign language service, our English service was not immune to good humour and fantasy. Our weekly Sunday Letterbox programme allowed us to reply on the air to listeners in distant countries. The contents was varied, from generous thanks to strong comments about the world's problems. Sometimes we were uncertain whether to take seriously the stories recounted.

A listener who signs himself Mr. Humdrum Hamstrung, wrote from a town called Sundry, in the Gongola group of islands in the Sargasso Sea between the West Indies and the Azores. He asks if it was true that a French prospecting company is to carry out a search operation on its cluttered shores. A quick look in a reference library to be sure that he was not pulling our legs! Sargasso is indeed a floating residue of marine life.

Back to our listener's letter, "The Gongolas, set in an oil-slick in the Sargasso Sea, have slumbered for generations as a totally independent monarchy. Rumour has it that the island's leaders are aspiring to become more independent, so that they could have their postage stamps printed abroad." At the time of replying to his letter, we had no further information on such an operation. We invited Mr. Hamstrung to write to us again with a reception report on our programmes. And we wished Mr. Hamstrung good listening to "All and Sundry!"

Chapter 10

"I have more recollections than if I were a thousand years old."

Charles Baudelaire

A PAGE IS TURNED; I have a new contract as Independent Producer of features for RFI, and a new home south of the river. No longer tied to office hours and a presence at the microphone to deliver the latest news, I was now free to work on chosen subjects to interest and inform overseas listeners in weekly half-hour programmes. Recorded features required research and preparation before broadcasting and marketing. The choice of subjects was wide, ranging from traditional and historic institutions to topical events reflecting French life and culture.

I began to assemble a list of potential subjects for my new mission, beginning with familiar monuments and institutions to interest future visitors to France. For example: how did the Palace of the Louvre become one of the world's most celebrated art museums; how did the Eiffel Tower survive calls for its destruction to become the symbol of France world-wide, and Notre Dame cathedral was not the earliest religious structure in the Gothic style in France.

Not all the guidebooks took the time or space to inform visitors that the Eiffel Tower was originally commissioned for the exhibition in 1889 for the centenary of the French Revolution. Conceived by the expert engineer Gustave Eiffel, the monument provoked violent protests over its original form. Celebrated personalities, such as Guy de Maupassant and the composer, Charles Gounod, described the tower as a "disgrace to Paris!" Charles Garnier, architect of the Paris Opera House, had called for its demolition at the close of the exhibition.

Taking a cue from the French writer and dramatist Jean Cocteau who wrote, "Foreigners know Paris better than we do," Paris had already emerged as the world's most visited tourist city when he expressed that sentiment. With more than 60 million foreign visitors annually, France was ahead of Spain, Italy, China and the U.S. The traditional image of Paris is perhaps the strongest attraction, even for the French themselves. More than one third of Parisian residents originally came from the French provinces.

Starting with France's best known museum, the Louvre, I talked to the General Secretary of the International Council of Museums, Elizabeth Departe, who announced a vast development project to renovate the once Royal Palace that began as a medieval fortress to defend fifty thousand Paris inhabitants. Declared a Royal Residence by King Philippe Auguste in 1204, the Louvre was opened to the public for the first time in 1793. The first art collection in the Palace was started by Francis I in the 16th century. By decree of the Convention of the First Republic, the collection was donated to the French people and had become the National Museum of France. The bicentenary year of the Louvre Museum was a celebration of its rich past and an opening on the future of the Grand Louvre.

My move from the fashionable sixteenth district of Paris to the "popular" Montparnasse quarter was an adventure. I had bought a small ground-floor flat in a quiet road between a busy market street and the second largest cemetery in Paris. It was a district of narrow cobbled streets, old apartment buildings and small homes with gardens jealously defended against local urban developments. From my window, I could see grass growing between the cobbled stones near where I parked my car. Several meters below this district of the city, the historic catacombs and ancient quarries attracted visitors to visit the source of stone once used to build early Paris. The labyrinth of underground passages became a secret refuge for the resistance forces during the war-time occupation of Paris. The quarter of Montparnasse had also acquired a reputation for artistic creation rivalling that of Montmartre. There was much to learn about my new quarter.

Bicentenary

As the months passed, the bicentenary of the French Revolution grew nearer and could not be overlooked. Three French Ministries and a bicentennial committee worked to give form and content to the event. The director of the Bicentennial Mission, Jean-Noel Jeanneney declared, "The legacy of the French Revolution is still very much alive. Our nation is rich in its memory and the roots of 20th century France are still its founding myth." President Mitterand, into his second seven-year term as Socialist President of France, saw the country as a key member of the European Community, maintaining France's leading geo-political role. Questions were asked if the twelve emerging states of the European Community could one day become as important as the United States of America.

The main commemorative events took place in the summer months of 1979, with exhibitions, conferences and pageants recalling the Revolution and reliving a major chapter of French history. Hundreds of semi-official and commercial events were planned, recalling the causes and consequences of the Revolution. The visiting public was invited to attend a round-table discussion in a huge tower erected in the Tuileries Gardens. Radio France International hosted a gathering of distinguished bilingual personalities present in Paris for the occasion. I was accepted to chair the English-speaking gathering and to present the participants. Actors, architects and tourist officials were briefed while radio technicians prepared to record the event.

While the world's media watched with curiosity, the annual influx of visitors began to arrive in France. Among the invited guests was the English architect, Peter Rice, who had collaborated with Renzo Piano, the creator of the Pompidou Centre. Rice was known in the profession as the "James Joyce of structural engineering!" He had also collaborated in designing the Australian Sydney Opera House. English-speaking visitors were pleased to put questions to the architect who had even contributed to the "wind-break" under the Great Arch at La Défense, visible from where we were gathered in the tower in the Tuileries Gardens.

The great arch of La Défense attracts new businesses.

Many countries associated themselves with the French bicentenary and representatives of all the American States were invited to attend the traditional Bastille Day parade down the Champs Elysées Avenue to affirm their common bond of Liberty. The July 14th parade was attended by an unprecedented number of official guests of the French President, including President George Bush and government leaders. Five thousand foot-soldiers including women in uniform, 700 motorised vehicles and a squadron of planes and helicopters swept over the Arc de Triomphe in close formation on the day to lay a curtain of blue, white and red vapour that drew applause from all who watched the demonstration in person or on television coverage worldwide.

Most official events were centred in Paris, including the inauguration of the new Paris Opera House at Bastille Square. The President also attended the International Federation of Human Rights and Sciences in the Arch of Man in the western Paris business quarter of La Défense.

A Capital in Evolution

The celebration of the Bicentenary of the French Revolution provoked renewed interest in Paris as a capital city. While its place in history was assured, the development of the city as an administrative centre and the seat of government had to be reaffirmed in relation to other capitals. Under President Mitterand, developments had taken place that would change the familiar aspect of the city known to the outside world. Among the projects included was the new glass pyramid greeting visitors to the entrance of the Louvre Museum, a new national library contained in four tower buildings on the southern banks of the Seine and the thirty-sixth bridge to span the river in Paris.

French leaders were anxious to protect the value of Paris as a focus of cultural and commercial activity. The new business centre of La Défense at the western edge of Paris had already become a pole of attraction. The new Euro Tunnel between France and Britain had brought Paris, Brussels and London closer together and two international airports north and south of the city were joined by a new fast road and rail links. Express rail connections and urban communications brought an ever-growing volume of visitors to the city. Projects such as the Pompidou Centre and the Louvre Museum offered a wider range of historic collections while the former Orsay rail terminus had become an art museum and cultural centre.

Like many capital cities, Paris suffered the problem of transporting workers and visitors. While the expanding Métro network brought tens of thousands into the capital each day, the city's buses had to compete with increasing traffic congestion from private automobiles and delivery services. Once, there had been single-decker buses with open platforms at the rear. Double-decker buses of the London pattern had been introduced but many Parisians declined to negotiate the narrow stairway. Another deterrent was the tree-lined boulevards where double-decker buses clashed with the growing branches of trees shading the motorway.

Successive French leaders sought to bring order to the development of the capital. While the original form of the city was threatened by growing suburbs, the former historic barriers and administrative limits had been overtaken by close suburbs. Paris had already added a wall of stone to its outer limits, which was not a rampart but a six-lane ring-road. The new highway called the Boulevard Peripherique, attracted motorists from two directions, from within the capital and from the outer suburbs. The new motorway replaced the old radial road system within Paris.

Newcomers can now choose their point of entrance or exit. The former old railway encircling the capital belonging to the French State railways has become an abandoned playground secretly explored by local youths. Only the Seine continues its course unperturbed by banks and quais. As the Latin emblem of Paris reminds us, "Fluctuat nec Mergitur" (The river flows but does not submerge the city.")

Epilogue

"It's out of Paris, that Paris, that I have carved my poems...and I have written more about you, Paris, than about myself: and more than from ageing, I have suffered from being without you."

Louis Aragon (1897-1982)

THE AMERICAN STATESMAN AND scientist, Benjamin Franklin, once stated, "Every civilised man has two homelands, and one of them is France." Paris was still emerging as a capital city when he expressed that sentiment. Today, statistics claim that Paris is the world's most visited capital. The traditional image of Paris is perhaps the strongest attraction even for the French themselves. Of the two million French residents of Paris, more than a third come from the French provinces.

The city of Paris owes its physical existence to the River Seine. The river used to flow past the foothill of Montmartre and a small tributary called The Bièvre flowed into Paris from the south. At the end of the 4th century the Gaullist town of Lutèce, at the intersection of the north-south Roman axis, became Paris, and the islands, the Ile de la Cité and the Ile Saint Louis, became the heart of the capital.

It is difficult to imagine what Paris was like before the Second Empire. It was certainly an insalubrious, plague-ridden city of narrow streets and rickety tenements. More than 300,000 people lived in the four central districts of the Right Bank of the river. In 1832 and 1849, there had been two serious outbreaks of cholera due to open street drains and lack of water. The Seine itself was unfit to drink and a source of pollution and infection.

At the inland junction of land and water communications, Paris became the focus of trade and cultural developments. The city offered moderate climatic conditions between northern excess temperatures and Mediterranean warmth. Other French cities such as Lyon, Marseilles, Bordeaux, possessed similar qualities, but none had the same allure and potential as "Paris sur Seine."

The city of Paris means different things to many people. Soldiers, artists, lovers, women of fashion and men of intellect, each find reflection of some part of themselves in the capital of France. To the French, Paris remains a separate part of France, defended, applauded, visited and revered, but purely French in character than the country that surrounds it. While a city like Paris is constantly evolving, efforts continue to define some fleeting aspect or larger truth about the relationships that produce a great city. Soldiers have defended her with ardour, writers and artists have coolly recorded its transient moods and noble aspects, while having their own personal affection for her. Though she is not young, she sometimes makes her appearance on a fresh spring morning when the air is clear and the slow flowing Seine sparkles below scudding clouds.

If one regrets the passing of some aspects of the city recorded in music and images, there are those who try to delve back to the spirit and times that produced them. Then Paris becomes young again, willing to be wooed and won by yet another generation of seekers after her eternal spirit. Paris offers the façade, the atmosphere for creative thoughts and actions, to relive the scene of a youthful conquest. Then the talk goes on at a café table far into the night beside the slow-flowing Seine.

As long ago as 1798, Napoleon declared, "If I were master of France I would want to make Paris not only the most beautiful city but also the most beautiful city that could exist!" However, the city of Paris as we know it today was largely the creation of one man, Georges Eugène Haussmann, a French Protestant of Alsatian origin. In 1853, Louis Napoleon Bonaparte, a nephew of the Emperor Napoleon and self-styled Napoleon III, personally chose Haussmann to be Préfet of the Seine in Paris, and commissioned him to carry out the rebuilding of the French capital. He conferred on Haussmann the title of Baron and gave him greater superiority and authority in the Senate for the work he was given. In the two decades that followed, Louis Napoleon and his Préfet transformed mediaeval Paris into a city of radial boulevards, impressive vistas and monumental facades.

During his seventeen years in office, Haussmann under Napoleon built nine new bridges and wharfs along the Seine, twenty churches, fourteen reservoirs and two aqueducts and the ten huge pavilions that became the Paris Central Food Market of Les Halles. The bringing of fresh water to the city, the creation of an efficient sewerage system and the establishment of parks and public gardens were among the improvements planned and carried out by Georges Haussmann. The two biggest public gardens, the Bois de Boulogne and the Bois de Vincennes owe their form and existence to Haussmann and Napoleon. Haussmann even recommended gas lighting for the city streets and a railway to encircle the capital.

What do newcomers find here and are they delighted in what they discover? Visitors often experience three periods of acceptance of what the capital has to offer. The first is the undoubted pleasure of seeing what one has long been familiar with in images and legends. The second period begins when one begins to detect the familiar faults and blemishes of other cities struggling to accommodate pressures of growth and development. The problems of an historic city in evolution can be painful. It takes time to recompose Paris as she really is. So then begins the period of acceptance of a city as it really is because you become part of it. Somewhere a balance has to be found between hopes and dreams and the acceptance of the realities of life.

At first, Paris appears to be like many other cities; buildings, statues, institutions, business and all the inherent handicaps of an urban agglomeration. The imposing strength and appearance of buildings give authority to its identity as the administrative seat of government and a State capital. Every structure is testimony of creative impulse and affirmation of authority. Churches, monuments, statues reflect determination and desire to create and endure. The result is a conglomeration of people and structures that express an identity of purpose and existence - the cradle of the French Republic.

The city of Paris is the product of energy, determination and love of creation. The generations of leaders who contributed to the multiple aspects of the city exercised their talents to leave a testimony of their presence. The American poet and writer, Lawrence Ferlinghetti, caught some of the mood Paris evoked in his poem "Birds-eye View."

Paris itself a floating dream
a great stone ship adrift
made of dusk and dawn and darkness -
dumb trauma
of youth!
such wastes of love
such wordless hungers
mute neuroses
yearnings & gropings
fantasies & flame-outs
such endless walking
through the bent streets

Thoughts on passing through Normandy from England, I recalled that armies have crossed these plains, battles have been fought, the wars dead lie in cemeteries. Villages stand silent. Church spires point to the sky as we rush towards the capital. What then is Paris?

Paris is a cobbled street with a bistro on the corner. Paris, a song sung by Chevalier and Piaf. Henry Miller wrote, "The streets sing, the stones talk, the houses drip history, glory, romance...." Paris has known war and occupation, tanks in the boulevards, bullets chipping ancient facades. Lights are reflected in the slow-flowing Seine, a reminder that nature has its way of keeping a balance between the past and the present.

Paris is Art and talking far into the night at a café table. Paris is a city of men of action, thinkers, idlers and women of elegance. Paris is also a small room high above the street where roofs stretch away to the East and the West. Paris is the Spring when the air is crisp with hope. It's the time when you say "Bon Jour" to neighbours and buy flowers for the one you are going to meet. Paris is memories of youth and love when the world was contained in a pair of eyes. Paris is a country where lovers are kings and youth pays homage to age. Paris is all you dreamed about because Paris was within you from the start.

Index

Apollo moon landing 27
Australian Broadcasting Commission 46

Bagnolet, France 2
Baker, Josephine 49, 52 - 55
        death of... 55
Belleville (Paris) 5
Bobino Theatre (Paris) 53 – 54

Café de la Paix 61 - 62
Chad 37 - 39
Chevalier, Maurice 6, 29-33
        death of... 36
Claire, René 36
Colette 75-76
Concorde (supersonic airliner) 11
Copenhagen 3
Cyprus 45
        (remembrance) 15-16

De Gaulle, Charles
        Quebec 10-11
        resigns 26
        veto 3
Dihya 59

Dumas, Alexandre 85
Durrell, Lawrence 14

Eaton boating song 65
Ellington, Duke 50 – 51

Ferlinghetti, Lawrence 101
Franklin, Benjamin 98
Fonteyn, Margot 66
French Bicentenary Anniversary 94
French film archives 46
French radio 9
French student revolt – 1968 21-22

Gance, Abel 48
Giscard d'Estaing, Valery 51 – 52, 65
Goudeket, Maurice 75-76
Guichard, Daniel 41

Haussmann, Eugène 99-100

International Herald Tribune 4
Ivory Coast 78-79

Jardin des Plantes 47

King, Jr., Martin Luther 20

La Défense 95
Langois, André 46
Laurel and Hardy 29
Les Halles market 40 - 41
        leaves Paris 35

Malraux, André 13, 46
Marceau, Marcel 83-85
Mastroianni, Marcello 50

mayor of Paris 88-89
Miller, Henry 101

Napoléon 99
Natural History Museum (Paris) 47
New York Times 4
Niger 37 - 39
Nureyev, Rudolf 66 - 67

Office de Radio Télévision Française (ORTF) 9, 57
Orwell, George 1

Pathé News 77
Piaf, Edith 6, 74 - 75
Paris
        developments 34 – 35
        evolution 96-97
        Les Halles 35, 40-41
        museums 47
        sounds of 47
Picasso, Pablo 63 – 64
Pompidou Centre 86-88
Pompidou, Georges
        death of... 51

Radio France Internationale (RFI) 57
        listeners letters 56, 91
Rice, Peter 94
River Thames at Eaton 65

Sartre, Jean-Paul
        Viet Nam war comments 20
Sauvage, Catherine 33
Shakespeare & Company 79-80
Statue of Liberty 69 - 71

Television, first 59 - 60

Turkey 45

United Nations, New York City 67 - 68
Van Gogh, Vincent 64
Vaughn, Sarah 49
Viet Nam war 20

Whitman, George 20, 80-81
Wilde, Oscar 62
World radio developments 11-12